HOLD FAST

TO YOUR

DREAMS

Passionate Desire
Turns Dreams into Reality

George Lee

4 MARCH 2013

GEORGE LEE MBE

Back Cover photo by Janine Waters

EVANGELISTA MEDIA™ srl
Via Maiella, 1
66020 San Giovanni Teatino (Ch) – Italy

"Changing the World, One Book at a Time."

This book and all other Evangelista Media™ and Destiny Image™ Europe books are available at Christian bookstores and distributors worldwide.

To order products, or for any other correspondence:

EVANGELISTA MEDIA™ srl
Via della Scafa, 29/14
65013 Città Sant'Angelo (Pe) – Italy
Tel. +39 085 4716623 • Fax: +39 085 9090113
Email: info@evangelistamedia.com
Or reach us on the Internet: www.evangelistamedia.com

ISBN 13: 978-88-97896-21-0
ISBN 13 EBOOK: 978-88-97896-22-0

For Worldwide Distribution, Printed in South Korea
1 2 3 4 5 6 / 15 14 13 12

BIRKHALL

10th September, 2012

Dear George

I was delighted to hear that you are writing a book, '*Hold Fast to your Dreams*', telling your own story. You have led, if I may say so, a most remarkable life, becoming World Open Class Gliding Champion at your first attempt in Finland in 1976, and then retaining the title against two subsequent challenges in 1978 and 1981. Your skills as a glider pilot were only too evident to me when I was fortunate to take to the skies with you in the June 1978 at Royal Air Force Bicester. This was my only experience of gliding and I enjoyed it enormously being instructed by such an expert, whose passion for gliding was only too obvious!

I know that your interest in aviation in general, and gliding in particular, was sparked at an early age when you were serving as a Halton Apprentice and that this led to commissioning in the Royal Air Force, before becoming a fighter pilot flying the Phantom aircraft, then a second career as a commercial airline pilot. I am delighted to hear that you are still gliding today in Australia – and passing on your encyclopaedic knowledge to the next generation!

I am sure your book will be an inspiration to others, and I just wanted to pass to you and Maren my very best wishes for a long and happy retirement.

Yours most sincerely

Charles

Dedication

To my wife, Maren, who has supported me through
so much over 43 years of marriage.

ACKNOWLEDGEMENTS

To Albert Johnson for his friendship and for his dedication and commitment as my crew chief for every World Gliding Championships in which I have flown, as well as for many other major national and international competitions.

To Amanda Wells, without whose encouragement and support this book would not have seen the light of day.

ENDORSEMENTS

I have been one of only a few to have experienced the privilege of flying with George Lee in both a Royal Air Force F-4 Phantom and in a glider. I recall just sitting back and admiring his ability to precisely do what he wanted with a flying machine. I have also witnessed his quite extraordinary skill in air-to-air gunnery, an art in which no one in the RAF came anywhere near equalling him. I have tried, in vain, to keep up with George on cross-country gliding flights whilst flying an identical type of machine; he has an ability to get the most out of often fickle air currents which left one wondering just how he did it. George has what they say in the trade: "a truly exceptional pair of hands". Besides this, he is the most modest of men and completely dedicated to all to which he turns. It has been my luck to have worked with and competed against a most remarkable pilot, whose achievements are unlikely ever to be repeated. If you seek inspiration, you need go no further than to read this book.

I D Macfadyen
Air Marshal
Constable and Governor
Windsor Castle

George Lee tells the story of his long and event-packed flying career in a straightforward style that will appeal to all. Born and educated in Ireland, George realised he wanted to be a pilot while still at school. As a first step towards his goal he joined the Royal Air Force as an Aircraft Apprentice. During this training he started gliding. His passion for this demanding and fascinating sport led him to win three World Open Class Championships and many other highly competitive soaring contests. He managed to integrate these outstanding achievements with a most successful career as an RAF officer and fighter pilot, and later as a Boeing 747 captain with Cathay Pacific Airways. After retirement from airline flying, he embarked on the ambitious task of setting up and running his own airfield and advanced soaring centre in Australia, aimed at helping young glider pilots to improve their skills. He and his wife, Maren, are now Australian citizens. This account of his life as a pilot clearly shows the determination, dedication, and concentration George has applied to achieve success during his remarkable flying career, as does his devotion to Maren and their two children. One is also left with the strong impression that he and Maren have drawn much inspiration from their Christian faith. The book will be of particular interest to those with a love for flying, and in the pressures and joys of competitive gliding at the highest level.

Air Vice-Marshal John Brownlow,
CB OBE AFC FRAeS
Former Chairman, RAF Gliding and Soaring Association

CONTENTS

FOREWORD

George Lee is probably the most focussed person I have ever met in life and has to be admired for his extraordinary application to the task in hand. Readers of this book will know him as a triple World Gliding Champion (Open Class), but many will not be aware that for a number of years he was an operational fighter pilot with the Royal Air Force flying F4 Phantoms where his application gave him the highest possible results. And in getting to that level, he did not have a straightforward ride and had to apply himself at every stage of his life to make the grade to become a Royal Air Force pilot; and not just any old pilot, but one of the very best. Although he writes about this in his book, his modesty has prevented him from making much of it—but I can and do so now. If ever there was a case of "pulling oneself up by the boot straps" then George is the perfect example.

But I really only know George from his gliding where his application is legendary. As a one time member myself of the British Gliding Team, I once asked him what the secret was that had made him achieve success well beyond my own rather meagre achievements, and I remember that he replied on the lines of, " I always set my sights on being World Champion and I knew I could achieve it". He believed in himself and what an example he set by so doing. Looking back I did not have such confidence in my own ability and that is probably the most important thing that George's success highlights.

Attention to detail is something else I recall so clearly and can be seen in this little snippet from a World Championship. At the end of each flying day, the wings of gliders taking part would have hundreds of squashed flies along the leading edge of the wings and one of the tasks of each crew at the end of each day would be to remove the aforesaid flies to ensure optimum performance was achieved at the start of the next day's competition. (This was in the days before "bug-wipers" had come on the scene). George's crew would deliberately leave just one fly on so that the next day, when George checked his glider, he would have the satisfaction of discovering and removing it! Attention to detail is another of George's characteristics that has set him apart from many others. The other one that is so relevant is that he was and is a superb pilot in the sense of being a "natural".

George, by his success in life of overcoming many obstacles and achieving his ambition, sets an example to all who aspire to achieve their own personal goals, and he also shows that one should strive for the utmost as only then will you discover what is really possible.

And, when his time in the Royal Air Force came to an end, I must mention his extraordinary application in achieving a first time pass in his ATPL (Airline Transport Pilot's Licence) sufficient to enable him to secure the one and only job available at the time with Cathay Pacific, and doing so in what must have been a near record time! Typical of him!

This book is inspirational and is a "must" for all glider pilots and to anyone who aspires to achieve something in life but sees nothing but obstacles in his or her path.

John Delafield
Air Commodore (RAF retired)
Eight times British National Gliding Champion

PREFACE

Dreams can be very powerful. Many dreams are without substance, even insignificant, but then there are the dreams that deeply impact the very core of our being. These are the dreams that we may experience repeatedly, the content of which keeps pressing into our thoughts and even our emotions.

This book is the story of my life so far, within which I have known the realisation of my dreams. The story starts with my early years in Ireland and the sowing of the seeds of desire to become a pilot. From my humble, non-aviation related beginnings in Ireland, the story continues with my joining the Royal Air Force (RAF) as an engineering apprentice and finally becoming a fighter pilot flying Phantoms.

I share how I took up gliding to show motivation towards becoming a pilot and how I was drawn towards competition gliding, the fascination contributing to my winning the first three World Championships that I entered, becoming the first person in history to do so. My story covers the time I took Prince Charles up for his first flights in a glider and my being subsequently invited to lunch with The Queen and Prince Philip at Buckingham Palace.

I describe how I met Maren, my Norwegian wife, and how we jointly made the big decision that I should exercise my option to leave the RAF at the age of 38 and face the bleak prospect of trying to secure employ-ment during the harsh recession of the early 1980s. The story continues with my acceptance into Cathay Pacific Airways and moving to Hong Kong to fly B747s for fifteen years.

I am a Christian, and *Hold Fast to Your Dreams* covers my coming to saving faith in Hong Kong, a faith that has become central in my life. Also covered is our joint decision to retire to Australia and set up ad-vanced coaching gliding courses in rural Queensland.

I have lived a varied and exciting life so far. There are people who say life is pre-determined and that's the way things are going to work out. I disagree because I believe that we have been given the freewill to make choices and decisions in every area of life and that we have to live with the consequences of those decisions.

Dreams and visions can be powerful, significant events in life, and it's good to meditate on them. The power of the mind is often under-estimated; but if we reflect on the content and implications of our dreams and visions, they can become reality providing we hunger for that outcome. I dreamed about becoming a pilot and that became a reality. When I discovered the challenge and satisfaction of competition gliding, I dreamed about winning the World Championships and that became a reality. During my final years in Hong Kong, I dreamed about setting up gliding courses for experienced junior pilots. I was given a vision of what the physical setup would look like, and it all became a reality as envisaged.

I wrote this book because I was given a wonderful opportunity to have my life story published. It is my hope that everybody who reads my story will be both encouraged and inspired to hold fast to their dreams for they have the potential to be truly life-changing.

Hold fast to dreams
For if dreams die
Life is a broken-winged bird
That cannot fly.

—Langston Hughes

Chapter 1

FISHING AND FLYING

Change brings opportunity.
—Nido Qubein

———◅◦▻———

The date was 27 June 1976. I was standing on the winner's podium at Rayskala in Finland having just won the first World Gliding Championships that I had entered. The partying had been long and hard the night before followed by little sleep, but there was no doubting the reality of what had happened. My dream had come true, and I was over the moon! The final day of the championships had been very challenging, but that was then—the next day was one of the proudest days of my life up to that point. The day was made all the more memorable by my then-pregnant wife being with me for the moment.

The dream had been birthed many years before, but I am getting ahead of myself, and I need to fill in the gaps.

I was born in Dublin on 7 November 1945. I have one sister, June, who is five years my junior. I grew up in a suburban area called Monkstown on the south side of Dublin Bay. During my early years, my father was a clerk in a clothing factory; later, he and my mother rented and ran a small shop selling ladies' and children's clothing. We didn't have much money; but we were a close family, and I have happy memories of my childhood years.

My mother came from a farm called Macreddin near Aughrim village in County Wicklow some 50 miles south of Dublin, and I used to spend my school holidays on the farm. It was a beautiful area with gently rolling hills, streams, and one major river. I was never too keen on the farm work, but I enjoyed fishing for trout and shooting rabbits with a .22 rifle. The nearest small town was about three miles away, and occasionally my uncle would treat me to a night at the local cinema to watch the inevitable Western. I have a clear memory of my uncle George setting off from the farm on his bicycle with me perched on the cross bar for what was never a particularly comfortable journey. The whole movie experience was entertaining in more ways than one as sometimes the bulb in the projector would blow, the spare had been used, and there would be a 45 minute interval as someone drove to the nearest larger town to get a replacement bulb.

There was a wonderfully simple but deeply satisfying rhythm to life on a small farm in those days. On Sunday mornings we would get dressed in our best clothes and make the 15 minute walk up to a small church located on the hillside. In typical country fashion, the locals would spend what seemed like an interminable amount of time putting the world to rights both before and after the service.

Christmas on the farm was a time of almost unbearable excitement for a young boy as the turkey, ham, and mince pies were prepared. The big kitchen always had a warm, welcoming atmosphere as the Aga cooker gave out its gentle wraparound heat. I remember indecently large Christmas puddings being prepared, wrapped in muslin, and suspended on hooks in the kitchen ceiling. The night before Christmas Day never involved much sleep as the excitement was too great. It took a particular effort to feign deep slumber as Santa Claus came into my bedroom to place mysteriously wrapped presents in the sock that hung from the end of my bed. Christmas Days were especially wonderful, starting with an early church service and then a whirl of opening presents in front of the magnificently decorated real Christmas tree, followed by a severe case of overeating overlaid with noisy talk and laughter. Not all of my school holidays were spent on the farm, but those that were gave the longest lasting memories.

———◦———

Back in Monkstown, my spare time was invariably spent either fishing or digging for fish bait as we lived in a small apartment about 100 metres from the sea. There were two local piers which gave protection for small craft as well as provided shelter for a terminal where ferries docked having come across the Irish Sea from Wales. My favourite fishing haunts were at various points along the western pier. Fishing in the '50s was very good, and I regularly brought home bags of mackerel, flounder, plaice, gurnard and codling. I have so many happy fishing memories, such as hooking fast-running mackerel on the rising tide at the end of the pier, and landing soft-biting plaice as I basked in the late afternoon sun on the western side of the pier.

Fishing didn't stop in winter, and many a dark cold evening was spent well wrapped up and equipped with a Thermos flask full of hot tomato soup as I fished for codling. I was not a very considerate angler as I insisted on bringing all my fish home to be cleaned out in the warmth and comfort of the kitchen. This gory practice had the unfortunate effect of putting my sister off eating most species of fish for life.

When I wasn't fishing, I would go down at low tide with my fork to dig for bait. The target species of bait were rag worm and lugworm, both of which could be up to 18 inches long. Particular care had to be taken with the rag worm as they had retractable pincer claws at the head which could give a nasty bite. Digging for bait was backbreaking work, but it was a satisfying part of the fishing cycle, even if keeping the bait at home pending the next fishing expedition was a further challenge to family relations!

Even if I wasn't fully aware of it at the time, important seeds were sown during my bait digging sessions. As I periodically took a rest, I would watch the seabirds as they soared along the rising air generated by the westerly winds blowing against the pier. I was both fascinated and captivated by this activity as the birds never needed to flap their wings;

it all seemed so effortless. The seeds started to germinate as I imagined myself doing what the birds were doing. I had regular vivid dreams that I was a soaring seabird skimming along the wave tops without flapping my wings. I can clearly remember those dreams even today.

Unfortunately, the fishing memories were not all good as a man who worked as a projectionist in a local cinema made contact with me on my visits to the pier and, in due course, he sexually molested me on a regular basis. He courted my favour by giving me presents from time to time including a fishing rod. I was too embarrassed to tell anybody what was going on.

———◦———

My primary education took place in a small church school in Monkstown. As my parents didn't have much money, it was a particularly satisfying experience to succeed in being awarded a scholarship to attend a major secondary school in Dublin called "The High School". This was a good school, and the quality of the educational foundation that I received made the daily commute worthwhile. Unfortunately, I was on the receiving end of some severe bullying and mocking, the adverse effects of which, combined with the earlier mentioned sexual molestation, remained with me for many years afterwards.

Amazingly, in spite of my undoubted slight physique, I was selected for one of the school rugby teams. I must have had an inspired day when I was selected, but I didn't have long to worry as I performed abysmally during my first match and was quickly dropped from the team.

I was somewhat of a loner during my childhood, and I didn't have many friends. One friend I did have decided that he was going to join the Royal Air Force (RAF) as an engineering apprentice. The aviation seeds within me had definitely germinated by this time even though there were no family members or friends who had any connection with flying. I decided that I wanted to be a pilot; and as I read the information that my friend had, I discovered that it was possible to be commissioned at the end of the apprenticeship, it being necessary to be an officer in order to become a pilot. I decided to make the same decision as my friend had made, but it was then necessary to fly to Belfast to sign the relevant papers, there being no RAF recruiting offices in the Republic of Ireland.

As my father was too busy running the shop, my uncle Sidney agreed to come with me, and we flew from Dublin to Belfast in an Aer Lingus Fokker Friendship. This was my first flight in any kind of aircraft, and I clearly remember feeling elated as the wings flexed and we became airborne; I definitely wanted to be a pilot! After a period of time, I received confirmation that I had been accepted for a three-year engineering apprenticeship, training to become an electrical fitter (air).

I know it must have been hard for my family, particularly my mother, but I left Ireland in January 1962 at the tender age of 16 to make my way to RAF Halton in southern England to become a member of the 100th entry of engineering apprentices. I had never been abroad before, and to say that it was a culture shock would be a gross understatement! Everything was different and, once the honeymoon period was over, I experienced the turning of the screw of military discipline. At the young age of 16, it was hardly surprising that I felt homesick and, as I was used to being a loner, I didn't make friends easily. However, it was a safe and secure environment with all basic needs provided, even if that didn't include the pleasures of home cooking. As all our needs were catered for, I didn't get paid very much; I recall receiving one pound (about $1.60 today) per week and managing to save half of it! We were accommodated in a large barrack block, each room having about twelve beds. Toward the end of my training, I was promoted to the rank of leading apprentice, and I was then given a room of my own at the end of the main room.

There was a wide range of hobbies and activities available for us at Halton and, not surprisingly, I chose to become involved with aero modelling. It was through this activity that I made a couple of good friends, Pete Miller and Chris Lewtey. We specialised in combat flying; that is, two of us would stand in the middle of a circle and at the end of our individual control lines we had powered flying wing models with long streamers trailing behind. The aim was to manoeuvre the model by means of the control lines into position behind the other model and use the propeller to cut off the opponent's streamer.

I have to admit that I wasn't very good at my primary trade as I was not and am not a technically minded person. I knew that it was possible to be accepted for commissioning at the end of the apprenticeship; but when I got to Halton, I discovered that I was one of approximately 160 apprentices and of that number only two or three would be selected for commissioning. As my technical work was poor, it was clear that I was not going to be one of those two or three! As I reflected on the error of my ways in committing to a three-year engineering apprenticeship, I wondered what I could do to improve my situation. It was at this point that I learned about the availability of gliding as the RAF Gliding and Soaring Association (RAFGSA) Centre was not far away at an airfield called Bicester. A small number of apprentices, notably Chris Gill and Terry Holloway, went there regularly at weekends. I decided to give it a try, reasoning that taking up gliding would show definite motivation towards becoming a pilot. My first flight in a glider was in a Sedbergh T21 basic side by side two seat trainer affectionately known as "The Barge". The date of my first glider flight was 3 March 1963, my instructor was Harry Jones, the flight took place in light rain, it lasted for three minutes and I was totally hooked! I knew at that moment that whatever happened in my professional life I would continue with gliding.

Bicester was a small airfield and a typical winch launch, that is being pulled up on a stranded steel cable, only gave enough height for a flight time of three or four minutes. I became independent with my transportation, acquiring firstly a scooter and later a motorbike enabling me to get out to Bicester on most weekends. My training progressed, and I went solo on my 49th flight on 23 June 1963 in a Grunau 2 single seater.

Being in command of any aircraft for the first time is a special occasion, and my first solo flight in a glider was no exception. There was a sense of joy in my heart as I savoured the freedom of flying alone and being responsible for every decision as well as for the safety of the glider.

Then I discovered the joy of soaring in thermals in the Grunau; on one of my early soaring flights in the glider, I became so preoccupied with the sheer pleasure of what I was doing that I lost all track of time. There was normally a flight time limit of one hour when local soaring so that others could get their share of the flying. Anyway, I was suddenly aware of the fact that I was not alone; the duty instructor had sent the Chipmunk up for me and Wing Commander (retired) Don Hanson came alongside, slid the canopy back and pointed downwards in a very clear manner—I got the message!

Andy Gough was the manager/Chief Flying Instructor at the RAFGSA Centre at the time and he was a legendary figure. Within the military rank structure he was a Warrant Officer, but he had such an imposing presence that he was known to make senior officers come around to his viewpoint remarkably quickly. He was unfazed by most things, but if you got on the wrong side of him, you certainly found out about it. Andy's deputy was Ron Newall, and together they made a powerful and experienced team. An example of Andy being unfazed about most things happened one day when, as the pilot in the Tiger Moth opened up the throttle to commence a tow, the propeller proceeded to detach itself from the aircraft and spin away sideways, fortunately without anybody being hurt. Andy had observed what had happened, and he just grunted, walked over to the sorry looking Tiger Moth, hoisted the tail of the aircraft onto his right shoulder and proceeded to walk it back to the hangar for rectification.

———◁◦▷———

As my ambition was to become a pilot, I was very aware that I needed to achieve the minimum educational requirements of five General Certificate of Education (GCE) Ordinary or "O" levels. My Irish educational certificates were not acceptable in this regard as I had left school before taking the Leaving Certificate which would have met the requirements. So, on top of all the studying that I had to do for the course at Halton, I also studied for and passed four GCE "O" level subjects. I somehow managed to graduate from the three-year apprenticeship at Halton with the rank of Junior Technician and, as we were the 100th entry, we had the honour of having Princess Alexandria at our passing out parade.

When it was all over, and in an act of rebellious defiance, I roared around the camp on my motorbike that I had been keeping in a lock-up garage in the local village—a bike that nobody in authority knew about and that I wasn't supposed to have according to the rules!

I had managed to get home to see my family in Ireland on a number of occasions during the three-year apprenticeship using the regular ferry service from Holyhead in Anglesey, but it was now time to change my professional location. In January 1965, I was posted to RAF Colerne, a military base near Bath in southwest England. My job was to work on the Hastings, a four piston engined tail dragger aircraft that was used in the transport and para-dropping roles.

Fortunately there was an active gliding club at Colerne, and I was able to continue with my flying nearly every weekend. The club name was the Bannerdown club, and it is still an active club albeit at a different location. The club had a winch-only operation, and there was a good fleet of club gliders.

An interesting privately owned glider that was based at the club was called the MD1, and it had a special fuselage but used KA6 wings. This glider was owned by Pete Lane who was small of stature so the cockpit was correspondingly tight; and although I had many enjoyable hours in this glider, there was never much in the way of spare room in the cockpit. The chief flying instructor of the gliding club was a Hastings pilot called Tug Willson, a man who was to play a very important part in my professional life. Although at this stage my professional life was not where I wanted it to be, my gliding gave me all the challenge and satisfaction that I wanted. I still had my trusty motorbike, a BSA 650cc Super Rocket, whose ultimate performance I tested periodically on the deserted main runway at Colerne during the quiet hours when nobody was around!

My gliding progressed steadily and I was cleared for my first cross-country flight, the weather finally coming good on 20 June 1965 when I flew the club's Olympia2b to Bicester, the airfield where I had my first flight in a glider. The Olympia range of gliders was produced by Elliott's of Newbury who primarily manufactured furniture! The only briefing I was given before takeoff was "Don't set off below 3,000 feet". I complied with this requirement, but my departure was followed by a long glide out down to 600 feet with a landing field selected! I managed to climb out of trouble and, having had that early scare, the rest of the flight was relatively uneventful.

There are a number of performance benchmarks laid down in gliding both to motivate and to reflect achievement. The A and B badges are awarded after the first solo flights, while the C badge is awarded after the first soaring flight. The next badge is the Silver C badge which has three components: a cross-country flight of at least 50 kilometres, a height gain of at least 1,000 metres (just under 3,300 feet) from the lowest point of the flight, and finally a flight duration of at least five hours. On that flight on 20 June 1965, I managed to achieve all three components of the Silver C badge, the only problem being that I was only permitted to claim two of them on any given flight according to the rules. I reasoned that the distance and duration components were the most demanding and that I would soon pick up the height component. In fact, it took another six weeks for me to complete my Silver C badge.

On the day that I got my Silver C height it wasn't possible to get sufficient altitude in clear air as the cloud base was too low. However, when thermals form what are known as cumulus clouds, the lift continues inside the cloud, usually with a greater strength than outside the cloud. The United Kingdom is one of the few countries in the world where glider pilots can legally fly in clouds as long as they are clear of controlled airspace. On the day of my flight, the cloud base was only 3,600 feet above ground, but I was able to climb up inside the cloud to 6,000 feet, thus completing my Silver C badge. If cloud flying is planned and executed responsibly, it can be a most rewarding and beautiful experience. The panorama on exiting the side of a large cumulus cloud into brilliant sunshine can be truly spectacular.

The next badge after Silver C is the Gold C badge which has two additional components to the five hours requirement: flying a cross-country distance of at least 300 kilometres and achieving a gain of height of at least 3,000 metres (just under 10,000 feet) from the lowest point of the flight. My first attempt at flying 300 kilometres was in July 1966 in a Skylark 4, but a major navigational error resulted in my being unable to make the claim even though I got back to Colerne and had flown in excess of 300 kilometres. My next attempt was in May 1967 when I successfully completed an uneventful 310 kilometres out and return flight in an Olympia 419 from an RAF station called Upavon.

The next qualification after the Gold C badge comprises three so-called "Diamonds". They are: 1) completing a declared 300 kilometre flight, 2) flying a distance of at least 500 kilometres, and 3) achieving a height gain of at least 5,000 metres (just under 16,500 feet) from the lowest point of the flight. My flight from Upavon therefore qualified me for one of the diamonds. During the time at Colerne, I also decided that I had sufficient gliding experience to be trained as an instructor and that it was time to put something back into the sport that I loved so much. So in August 1967 I returned to Bicester to be put through the mill for a few days and emerged still smiling as a qualified instructor.

A proud RAF Apprentice
in best uniform.

Chapter 2

LIVING, LOVING, LEARNING

A mind that is stretched by a new experience
can never go back to old dimensions.
—Oliver Wendell Holmes Jr.

———◦———

A major event in my life took place during my time at Colerne—I met my future wife, Maren, at a Halloween party at the gliding club. Maren is Norwegian, and she was staying with a local farmer and his family who were friends of Maren's parents. Maren had come over from Norway to spend some time in England with the intention of improving her English. The farmer was a special member of the gliding club because of his engineering expertise, and it wasn't long before this resulted in Maren visiting the club.

I was always busy when flying was taking place—either instructing, driving the cable retrieve tractor, or driving the winch. Maren commented years later that I never seemed to take a break and come into the launch point bus to sit down and have a cup of tea. It might have taken a Halloween party to get us together, but we were destined to meet; and for me, it was truly a case of love at first sight.

Life had been fairly straightforward for me at Colerne up to this point, but now I was courting! Maren must have seen something in me that she liked as our dates weren't always the most romantic occasions;

for example, I remember taking her on the back of my motorbike to the cinema in the pouring rain. We met in October 1966, and I took Maren to Ireland for Christmas the same year to meet my parents; I could be described as a fast mover!

We went to Norway in June 1967 on my motorbike with a suitcase strapped on the back, and I met Maren's parents for the first time. The suitcase stayed on the back of the motorbike *most* of the time. I might have been a bit aggressive in my handling when we went round the final roundabout before boarding the ferry as the suitcase went shooting off sideways. Fortunately any damage was only cosmetic. For part of the time in Norway, Maren and I went on a camping trip with the motorbike, staying at some unbelievably beautiful locations.

I managed to plan the route to go via the Norwegian Gliding Centre at Notodden to see if there was any chance of getting a flight. When I presented myself and my gliding logbook to the instructor on duty, I was somewhat surprised to be offered a Blanik all-metal two seater to take Maren for a flight, all without even a briefing. I must have looked trust-worthy. We had a thoroughly enjoyable flight that lasted for more than an hour as we enjoyed both ridge and thermal lift.

After our return to the farm, there was much family social activity in true Norwegian tradition, and an amusing incident occurred during one of the get-togethers. We were all seated around various sizes of tables, and I was sitting next to Maren's younger sister. It is Norwegian custom to hand the plate of food to the person who is seated next to you so that they can serve themselves. Maren's sister handed a plate of food to me and thought that she was inviting me to help myself, when in fact, instead of saying, "Help yourself", she was saying, "Behave yourself"! Needless to say, that managed to attract Maren's attention, as she wondered what I had been getting up to under the table!

At the end of our wonderful time together in Norway, I set off alone on my motorbike from Maren's home farm to return to England in a somewhat teary state. Maren stayed on in Norway to complete a six-month domestic training course.

On the professional front, I worked on the electrical equipment that was fitted to the Hastings, in the servicing bay as well as on the aircraft. It was demanding work in many ways as the aircraft were aging, and this was reflected in the condition of both the equipment and the wiring. Overall the aircraft did effective service, but a long shadow was cast one day when there was a fatigue failure in the area of the tailplane causing a loss of control and subsequent crash with multiple fatalities. The whole fleet was immediately grounded pending an in-depth investigation.

I was posted to nearby RAF Lyneham where I worked on the Comet jet transport aircraft for some months until the Hastings aircraft were cleared to resume operational flying. In spite of the aging fleet, I have some happy memories of being involved with the Hastings. I got to see different parts of the world, such as Newfoundland and the Bahamas where the meagre allowances allowed the purchase of one drink that had to last all evening! I also got to see Asmara in what is now Eritrea and spent some wonderful weeks in Kenya, involved in service associated with the oil embargo of Rhodesia. I had never been beyond the British Isles before seeing these places, and when I got to Kenya, I thought that I had died and gone to heaven! The air at an altitude of around 5,000 feet was like wine, and the flowers and the wildlife blew me away. I loved the great outdoors; but unfortunately, I overdid the sun exposure and ended up in hospital with bad sunburn.

Just after a year at Colerne, I took and passed the final GCE "O" level subject required to be accepted for commissioning. Tug Willson now came into the professional frame of my life. As I have intimated, I wasn't very good at my primary job and my assessment reports must have reflected that. I was, however, quite good at gliding, and Tug knew that my ultimate dream was to become a pilot. I needed to be accepted for commissioning before I could become a pilot, and Tug took it upon himself to speak up for me at station level so that my application to become a pilot could get off station. When that happened, I was called to go to RAF Biggin Hill for pilot aptitude and medical assessment tests, as well as extensive interviews.

I was now where I wanted to be, and I actually enjoyed everything that took place, being happy to paddle my own canoe. Everything went as expected, and I commenced officer training at RAF South Cerney in Gloucestershire a few months after returning from Norway. The training all went well, and I had the honour of commanding the passing out parade. There was a cocktail party at the end of the training, and I wrote to Maren asking her if she could come from Norway to attend, not having great expectations of a positive response. To my great surprise and delight, the answer came back that she would be coming! This plan greatly impressed the other girls at the domestic school!

My initial flying training started in December 1967 at RAF Church Fenton in Lincolnshire on the Chipmunk, a piston-engined tail dragger tandem two-seat trainer with good handling qualities. The training only lasted two weeks, and in February 1968 I started my basic pilot training at Number 3 Flying Training School, RAF Leeming in Yorkshire on the Jet Provost Mark 3 and 4, a nose-wheeled side by side single-engined jet trainer. The course was long and hard but at the end of November 1968, I was unbelievably proud to receive my RAF pilot wings. I knew just how important this course was, so I decided to put my gliding on the backburner for the duration of the course, apart from some Easter flying with the club at Colerne. The long drive from Leeming to Colerne was a memorable one as a fellow student offered to take me down in his immaculate soft top MGTF. I have this memory of driving down the motorway with the soft top flapping in the wind and rain, only some of which it kept out, and my driver singing joyfully as he twirled the ends of his classic RAF-style moustache.

My nose to the grindstone approach paid off handsomely as I was awarded four of the six available prizes as well as collecting the Sword of Honour for top student. The flying had been challenging but very satisfying. The instructor who did most of my flying training was Paul Sowman who found his relaxation in playing the classical guitar. He subsequently left the RAF and flew B747s with British Airways.

Maren was now back in the United Kingdom having completed her domestic course in Norway. We met up in London, and we became officially engaged in January 1968 as I gave her the ring that I had been able to purchase following the sale of my beloved motorbike—I must have been in love! Maren had secured a position with Foyle's bookshop in London, and she somehow managed to survive on the almost insultingly meagre salary of £8 (about $12.62 today) per week.

She stayed in the Norwegian YWCA, and whilst there she heard about a position that was available working with the Norwegian Shipping Office in London. She applied for the position, got the job, and her salary went up to £15 per week. Along with two other girls, Maren had had enough of the YWCA, and around the middle of the year the three of them rented a small apartment over Hammersmith underground station. We managed to see each other occasionally during the year and continue our courtship. I remember staying at her apartment on one visit to London and, on getting up from my sleeping position on the floor of the living area, asking her and the other girls how they managed to get any peace, never mind sleep! It's amazing what humans can get used to and the degree of noise that can be tuned out; they weren't aware of the noise. Those were financially challenging times for Maren, and sometimes she had to choose between buying a tube of toothpaste and getting a pair of tights, but it was valuable training for our early months of marriage.

We decided to get married on 7 December 1968. Maren went back to Norway in November to collect all her stuff, the journey itself being somewhat more than a routine travel experience. She managed to get approval from the shipping office to travel to Norway on a small cargo ship with the sick bay being her accommodation. As they traversed the North Sea, a bad storm brewed up, and the sea became extremely rough. Although she was sick, Maren survived the journey in good shape. However the news about the storm created a great deal of concern for her parents and family. Finally the small ship got within radio range and Maren was allowed to use the radio to reassure her parents that all was well.

December was in the middle of the busiest time of the year for my parents in the shop in Ireland, and they just couldn't leave everything and go to Norway for the wedding, so it was decided that it would take place in Ireland. Maren's parents came over from Norway with one of her three sisters and a brother in law. We were married in our local Church of Ireland church in Monkstown, followed by a formal reception in a nearby hotel. I made the foolish mistake in my speech of promising Maren's parents that I would be able to speak Norwegian the next time we met; that was one of the few promises in my life that I didn't keep.

Our "honeymoon" consisted of spending two nights in a lovely Irish country hotel before returning to England. We then managed to purchase a second hand car, a Ford Anglia, and we started married life in a small apartment in Shrewsbury, Shropshire, where we stayed for a few months before moving to Anglesey in northwest Wales to commence advanced flying training. There was a backlog within the flying training system, and I spent those few months in Shropshire flying Vampires from RAF Shawbury where the school for training air-traffic controllers was located. I enjoyed flying the Vampire although, as I am 6 feet 2 inches tall, there was little in the way of spare room in the cockpit.

Those were happy days, but our finances were incredibly tight. The RAF in its wisdom had decided that an officer was insufficiently mature to get married until the age of 25 and that anyone who got married before that age would not be paid marriage allowance. Maren's financial training in London paid off handsomely as we somehow managed to survive during those months. Although they were generally pleasant days, there was one note of sadness when there was a knock on the door one evening and I opened the door to see a policeman standing there. He had come to give me the unexpected news that my father had just passed away from a brain haemorrhage. He had been in some pain for a while, but it was still a shock to learn that he had died at the age of 52. In spite of our precarious financial situation, I managed to travel back to Ireland to attend the funeral and give support to my mother.

And so on to Anglesey in April 1969 to commence advanced flying training at Number 4 Flying Training School at RAF Valley. As I was still under the age of 25, Maren and I were not entitled to live in a married quarter, so we searched around the local area to find suitable accommodation. We ended up deciding on an old brick built house with a lot of charm called "Ty Croes Bach". It was at the end of a narrow country lane in the middle of the island—no one could say that we didn't have privacy!

The advanced flying setup was split in two sections, the larger part utilising the Folland Gnat, a small single engined tandem two seater with a phenomenal rate of roll, and the smaller section using the larger Hawker Hunter. It was decided that, due to my back length, I would not fit into the Gnat, so all of my advanced training would be done on the Hunter. I was not too upset about this as the Hunter had tremendous pedigree and was a beautifully stable aircraft to fly. The Hunter training section was located on the quiet western side of the airfield; we had a great boss, and in many ways it was run as a normal squadron.

I received the initial part of my training on the T7 Hunter, a side-by-side two seater, the engine of which produced adequate if not overwhelming thrust. After fourteen flights, I was let loose on the single seat F6 Hunter. The Valley F6 Hunters were affectionately known as GT6s as certain operational equipment had been removed from them, being superfluous for the training role. This reduction in weight, coupled with an engine that produced significantly greater thrust than the T7 engine, resulted in impressive performance. On my first flight in the F6, I seem to recall catching up with the aircraft as I passed 10,000 feet in the climb! I have wonderful memories of flying the Hunter; not only was it very stable in flight, but the handling was superb. There is a saying in aviation: "If it looks right, it usually is right", and the Hunter certainly proved that saying as it just looked right.

I got on well with my regular instructor, Hammy Armstrong, and the flying was demanding but exhilarating. The syllabus incorporated the full spectrum of advanced training, covering such areas as high and low-level flying, flying in formation and night flying. I particularly enjoyed the low-level flying over land as most of it was conducted at 250 feet above ground at speeds of up to 450 knots (just over 800 kph or 500 mph) and the routing was largely over the dramatic scenery of the Welsh mountains and valleys. There were only seven of us doing our advanced training on the Hunter, and we were a close-knit bunch; but my competitive nature got the better of me during the course. I tried too hard to prove that I was the best, and I ended up having a breakdown. I was taken off flying and sent home for a time in order to recover.

These were hard days for Maren as the event was totally unexpected, and she was unsure as to how to handle the situation. Fortunately it didn't take me long to recover, and I got stuck back into the flying. Somehow, in spite of this major hiccup, I was awarded the Cup of Honour at the end of the course. Understandably, Maren and I had our own individual mixed emotions as we left Anglesey. The flying had been superb, but I learned a valuable lesson the hard way. For Maren, our choice of accommodation, although charming and located in a beautiful area, was too remote, and she had endured too much loneliness over the four-month period of training.

We now faced an interesting situation. The training backlog had become more acute, and I was looking at a full year before I would commence my tactical and weapons training at RAF Chivenor in Devon. I reasoned that I would prefer to spend the year at a location where I would prefer to be rather than where the RAF might send me. I contacted the chief flying instructor, Andy Gough, at the RAFGSA Centre at Bicester and apprised him of the situation. Andy swung into action in his inimitable way, and it took very little time for my posting to Bicester to be approved! What a joy to get paid for combining powered flying with my beloved gliding for a whole year.

The reality was that it was a very demanding year. I did a lot of flying in the Chipmunk towing gliders and running the innumerable gliding courses, fortunately interspersed with a reasonable amount of solo gliding. Life did tend to become a bit of a blur from time to time, but one memory stands out. I was running a soaring course, and one of the pilots on the course went off for a flight, having been briefed to stay within gliding range of Bicester. He managed to drift off downwind in a weak thermal and ended up landing out. I was furious and, grabbing a tow-rope, I jumped into the Chipmunk and went off to find him. I did find his landing field which seemed to me to be ok to tow out of. It needs to be understood that I was not checked out for such an operation, but I was so annoyed that didn't feature in my thinking. Anyway, my landing went well, and the pilot and I pushed the glider into the farthest corner of the field, that is after we had a one-sided conversation from which he gained a clear understanding of how I felt about the whole situation.

Fortunately the take off and climb out from the field all went well, and we returned to Bicester without further incident. It was then a case of the pilot having to face a severe dressing down from Andy with me in attendance. The realisation of what I had done was now beginning to sink in, and I fully expected to receive a private debriefing from Andy after he had finished with the other pilot. I was delighted and relieved when I heard Andy telling the pilot how fortunate it was that I had been able to come and retrieve him by air!

One of the more interesting gliders that I flew during the year at Bicester was the BS 1, owned by Don Hanson. This was a high perform-ance glider during the 1960s, being 18 metres in wingspan and equipped with flaps. An interesting aspect of the cockpit design was that the pilot flew in an almost supine position, the aerodynamic thinking of the time being that the fuselage should be kept to as small a profile as possible. Flying in this position and looking ahead between the feet took a bit of getting used to, and early flights resulted in a degree of neck stiffness until eventually I was able to relax. Unfortunately there were only ever twenty BS 1s produced, and in 1963 the designer was killed when the aircraft suffered structural failure during a test flight.

At the other end of the performance spectrum, I managed to get a flight in a so-called Primary glider that had been built by the British company Slingsby Sailplanes. The design was based on the pre-World War II German SG 38 Primary glider that was intended to give prospective glider pilots an introduction on a type that was relatively easy to fly and, importantly, was easy to repair as there were likely to be landings that varied from heavy to crashing! Although this glider was towed up by powered aircraft at Bicester from time to time, my flight was from the winch.

If you are a reader who knows nothing about gliding, it needs to be understood that this machine was basic in the extreme, having no cockpit as such and no instruments. The pilot strapped himself on to a chair type of seat and was completely open to the elements. The performance was minimal, and I was briefed to remain inside the airfield boundary—good advice. The winch launch was pretty exciting, and towards the top of the launch I thought I would have a quick look down at the winch. I looked down between my boots and saw the bowed steel cable leading into the winch cab and the eyes of the winch driver looking up at me—I quickly looked back at the horizon! A brief circuit followed and the uneventful touchdown was followed by the shortest of ground runs as the main skid absorbed the energy in an effective manner. The major gliding event of the year at Bicester was that I got to fly in my first gliding competition. The event was the annual inter-services competition, and I was thrilled to end up winning my class—I was hooked!

On the domestic front, although I was not yet 25, there were a number of surplus married quarters at Bicester. For the first time in our married life, Maren and I were able to live on base. We also managed to enjoy what was basically a belated honeymoon when we went on holiday to Tunisia. Maren worked for most of our year at Bicester, first as a shop assistant in a department store in Oxford and then as a clerk at a local Ministry of Defence facility. She commuted to her second place of work on a Honda 50cc two stroke mini motorcycle. Another personal memory from this time was that the earlier mentioned Paul Sowman had left the RAF and needed to be trained to get his civil aviation license at the local major training centre at Kidlington. He wondered if Maren and I would be willing to accommodate him and his wife, Barbara, while the training was progressing; of course we were happy to assist.

Basic flying training
at RAF Leeming.

Our big day,
7 December 1968.

Chapter 3

Phantom Flying

*Choose a job you like and you will never have
to work a day in your life.*
—Confucious

———◄◦►———

I felt exhausted by the end of the year at Bicester, but there was no time for recuperation as Maren and I headed off for me to get some refresher flying on the Jet Provost before going to RAF Chivenor in Devon for my much delayed weapons and tactical training on the Hunter.

Although I was now over the magic age of 25, Maren and I were still not able to live in a married quarter at Chivenor due to my student status. Not having learnt the lesson from Anglesey, I signed the contract for a rambling old farmhouse in the middle of nowhere! Maren found the days at Chivenor to be hard going as not only was the accommodation remote, but we were there through the winter months.

As far as the start of the flying was concerned, it was a case of straight in at the deep end. The refresher flying on the Jet Provost had been inadequate as a preparation for the challenges of the Hunter flying. There was no slack in the system to make allowance for the fact that inexperienced pilots had gone for a year without flying fast jets, and there were a number of pilots who fell by the wayside during the early stages of the training.

The first flights at Chivenor were extremely challenging as many layers of rust were rapidly shed, but I was excited—at last I was being trained to become a real fighter pilot! The syllabus progressed from initial general handling through high-level and low-level formation flying, gunsight tracking exercises, air-to-ground weapons delivery and air-to-air combat. I enjoyed the air-to-ground weapons work the most because I happened to be fairly good at it! There was an air-to-ground firing range not far from Chivenor, and I got to drop bombs, fire rockets and use the Hunter's powerful built-in 30mm cannon. All in all, the course was a real workout, but I was aware of my skill and confidence levels increasing as it progressed; and all too soon it was over.

The decision was made that I would go on to fly the Phantom; operationally and fortunately, there was only a short break between the end of the Chivenor course and the beginning of the Phantom conversion course.

—◇—

Yet again Maren and I were on the move, this time to RAF Coningsby in Lincolnshire in 1971 where I was to learn how to fly the Phantom. It was good that a couple of friends who had been with me through the Valley and Chivenor training were still with me for the Phantom conversion. As I was still a student, Maren and I were not entitled to apply for a married quarter on base, but we were a lot more careful this time with our choice of accommodation!

It was quite a change going from the Hunter to the Phantom. The Phantom FGR 2 was a larger aircraft designed for a two-man crew, and it had two engines as opposed to the Hunter's single engine. The Phantom was designed as a medium to high-level interceptor, and it was equipped with a capable air-to-air radar that also had a reasonable lookdown performance. It was a very versatile aircraft, and the RAF used it in the three roles of air defence, ground attack and reconnaissance. In the air defence role, the Phantom carried the Sparrow radar guided missile and the

Sidewinder infrared tracking missile. The aircraft carried a very capable external pod for the reconnaissance role.

In the ground attack role, it carried the traditional mix of bombs and 68mm SNEB rocket pods as well as an effective gun. There have been a number of different models of the Phantom over the years, some of which had an internally mounted gun, but the models that the RAF used had an externally mounted gun pod. The gun was multi-barrelled, electrically fired and worked on the Gatling gun principle firing 20mm shells. It was very smooth in its operation compared to the high recoil of the 30mm cannon that was internally fitted to the Hunter. The rate of fire for peacetime use was 4,000 rounds per minute, but this could be brought up to 6,000 rounds per minute in war. It was a phenomenally accurate weapon, somewhat too accurate for air-to-air work where it is good to have a spread of coverage, especially using a basic non-smart gunsight.

The Phantom was not the most stable of platforms for air-to-ground use, particularly when compared with the Hunter which was a delightfully stable weapons platform. However, initial comments from experienced Hunter pilots became less unflattering about the Phantom as experience was gained. A number of pilots who had gone through earlier training with me were also on the conversion course. A new dimension was of course the navigator! The staff left it up to the students initially to sort crew pairing out, and I became crewed with a highly professional navigator called Phil Leadbetter. Although the operation was a standardised one, there was no doubt that there were notable advantages in having so-called constituted crews as each pilot and navigator got used to each other's operation and foibles. The conversion course lasted from June to October 1971 and, as I expected, was extremely demanding.

At the end of the course, Phil and I were posted to Number 6 Squadron which was also conveniently located at RAF Coningsby—finally we were ready for operational service. What a squadron to be posted to for my first tour of duty! The specialist role of the squadron was night ground attack. Ground attack by day was challenging enough but to do it by night elevated the challenge and difficulty to a whole new level. There were a number of live firing ranges spread around the United Kingdom, and much of the night ground attack work was done on these ranges. One of the more exciting ranges was Otterburn in the hills of Yorkshire. We would set off from Coningsby as a five aircraft formation and transit at low level in radar trail to commence our attack run.

The crews of the lead two aircraft specialised in delivering powerful Lepus flares that descended under built-in parachutes. The remaining three aircraft were the attackers. I have clear memories of pulling up and searching intently within the flare's circle of light to visually acquire the so-called "airfield" target. This was no mile and a half long runway; rather, it was a ploughed strip on the side of a hill, and accurate weapons delivery proved to be an immense challenge. Apart from the somewhat hairy nights at Otterburn, weaponeering at the coastal ranges was generally fairly straightforward, although still very demanding flying.

It has to be accepted that flying is a potentially dangerous activity at the best of times, and I had my own heart-accelerating moment on a daytime low level simulated attack profile. Much of our day flying involved planning and executing simulated attack runs against selected targets that were located within the designated low flying areas. We would select a prominent visual feature and commence our attack run on an accurate heading and speed for a calculated time before pulling up, rolling over, visually acquiring the target and carrying out a simulated weapons delivery.

On this particular occasion, following the pull up, I was unable to see the target until a late stage when I realised that I had overshot. I pulled the aircraft around and carried out the attack profile. It was all too rushed and what I hadn't realised was just how much speed I had lost during the extended positioning manoeuvre. I commenced the recovery pull up at the normal altitude but, because of the reduced airspeed, the aircraft didn't respond as expected. Speed is life in the aviation business, particularly so in the high performance fighter world, and I was not in a good position. The aircraft was "mushing" towards the ground; I selected full reheat to give me maximum available thrust. That did the job, but the ground came much closer than I had wanted to see, and it took some time for the heart rate to settle down!

———◆———

Occasionally we combined a simulated attack profile with bombing work on one of the ranges. Squadron procedure on simulated attack runs was to make all the switches as if it was a live attack, and on one particular day this was the scenario. The problem came when I made all the switches on the simulated attack run against a bridge in a remote (fortunately) area of northern England, resulting in the 28lb practice bomb being released. It was a quiet cockpit on the way home and, after engine shutdown, my navigator, Canadian Chuck Wierleychuk, jumped out of the cockpit and bent under the bomb carrier only to see that the bomb had indeed gone. Fortunately nobody had been injured in the area of the simulated target.

Another incident that took place on the squadron was very tragic. I was part of a formation of aircraft that had transited at high level to let down and conduct a low level mission in Wales. The weather conditions deteriorated markedly towards the end of the route, and the formation leader prudently called the low level mission off, ordering a climb out to high level for the return to Coningsby. When visual contact with the ground is lost, the first priority is to point the nose skywards and then get the aircraft turning onto the desired heading. For whatever reason, the pilot of one of the other aircraft got it the other way round, at least to some degree.

The procedure for safely pulling out and regrouping at higher level was for each crew to transition from visually navigating and flying in formation to going heads down and ensuring safe separation by acquiring the other aircraft on radar. During the pull out and having acquired all the aircraft on radar, suddenly one of the radar returns disappeared. My heart sank when there was no answer from the crew in response to the leader's radio calls. It was indeed a sad return to Coningsby that day to receive the news that the missing aircraft had impacted the side of a Welsh hill and that both crew members had been killed.

We all knew that flying was a potentially dangerous activity, but we loved what we did and accepted the inherent risks. Being young brings with it a sense of invulnerability; but when you lose two precious comrades, the risks are really brought home. A funeral service was held shortly afterwards, the loss of two colleagues being marked by the overflight of Phantoms in a "missing man" formation.

———◦———

If night ground attack was a new activity for me on joining 6 Squadron, air-to-air refuelling was a new challenge and skill that I had to learn. Air-to-air refuelling was an important part of squadron life, both when participating in large scale exercises some distance away from base as well as when transiting to other parts of the world.

There are two main methods for carrying out air-to-air refuelling. The American system is for the receiving aircraft to fly into position behind the tanker aircraft; an operator seated at the rear of the tanker controls the positioning of the refuelling boom onto the point of contact on the receiving aircraft so that fuel can be transferred.

The British system is that the receiving aircraft extends a retractable probe which is typically close to the pilot's head. The pilot then manoeuvres the aircraft into a close formation position behind the tanker aircraft which has extended the refuelling hoses. At the end of each hose there is a conical drogue or basket and the aim is for the receiving aircraft to slowly move forward and try to position the probe so that it will enter the conical basket and make contact with the valve at the end of the basket. If contact with the valve is made with sufficient force, the valve will open and fuel flow will commence. The pilot of the receiving aircraft then needs to hold the same position behind the tanker until the transfer is complete; he can then move slowly back until contact is broken and the probe can be retracted.

We carried out our air-to-air refuelling with the Victor fleet of tankers, the aircraft having been modified from its original V bomber role. The Victor had three air-to-air refuelling hoses, one extending from a pod on each wing and the third being a larger and heavier centreline hose. The wing hoses gave a lower rate of fuel flow than the centre hose; they were also more demanding to make contact with than the centre hose.

As the Phantom was moved forward, the combination of the aerodynamic wash from the Victor's wing and the influence of the Phantom's nose resulted in the drogue moving sideways at a late stage in the proceedings. This known event had to be allowed for when initially positioning before moving forwards. When a pilot got it right, the drogue moved sideways and contact was made. This late stage movement of the drogue was much less evident with the centreline hose as it was heavier and there was no aerodynamic influence from the wings. For the beginner, air-to-air refuelling has to be one of the most frustrating of skills to learn. A lot of time is spent moving forwards, missing the basket and dropping back to try again.

Needless to state, there was an extra dimension of challenge when carrying out air-to-air refuelling at night—but the greatest challenge of all was air-to-air refuelling when in clouds. Not only was there no natural horizon to refer to, but clouds often meant turbulence! The turbulence would cause the hose to dance wildly and it was very much a shot in the dark as to where it would be at the critical point when the receiving aircraft's probe arrived looking for fuel. Occasionally an aircraft on joint exercise with the navy a long way from home would have to return to base having reached a critical fuel state and not having been able to make contact with the tanker, definitely damaging to professional pride!

The implications of not being able to make contact with the supporting tanker were more serious when transiting to another country as it would mean diverting to an unfamiliar airfield in a foreign country with many ensuing complications. Squadrons regularly deploy to other countries for training, and 6 Squadron went to a base on Sardinia, Italy, annually for concentrated weapons training. The weapons range was Cape Frasca on the west coast of the island, and it was just a short transit from our host Italian military base of Decimomannu.

Squadrons become different organisations when they deploy overseas. There is a feeling of freedom from the daily pressures of the home base, and the result is a greater degree of cohesion and unity towards the achievement of the declared goals.

Cape Frasca presented some special challenges of its own! There were no particular issues with regard to day ground attack missions, but 6 Squadron's specialist role was night ground attack and that is where the issues arose. The Italian range staff were not too keen on working at night, and all kinds of pretexts would be given for the non-availability of the range, such as the sea state was too rough or the rescue vessel was unserviceable. They prevailed for a time, but our boss, Wing Commander John Nevill, was a very determined man, and he managed to tip the scales so that we got to do our night ground attack work.

My tour of duty with 6 Squadron lasted from November 1971 until April 1974, and I was involved with squadron detachments to various bases in Europe, particularly Germany and Italy. Two major deployments to Singapore were particularly special. The first time was in April 1972 and, with air-to-air refuelling support, we routed via Masirah in Oman, the island base of Gan in the Indian Ocean, and then on to the Singaporean air force base of Tengah.

The second deployment to Tengah was one year later; this time we routed via Akrotiri in Cyprus, Dubai in the United Arab Emirates, again to Gan, and on to Tengah. These trips involved significant air-to-air refuelling, fortunately all successful! Individual leg times were up to five hours which may not sound too long, but it was always good to get out of the cockpit at destination as the ejection seats were distinctly on the firm side. During these long transits, the tanker crews handled all the radio calls with Air Traffic Control so we were on a quiet "chat" frequency. The navigation was also handled by the tanker crews so there was little to stimulate the mind apart from looking at the unfolding scenery and anticipating the sandwich that constituted the body's in-flight refuelling. Of course there was also the challenge of having a toilet break whilst strapped on to an ejection seat, but I won't go into too much detail here except to say that we were supplied with heavy duty sponge-filled lockable bags.

My navigator and I did have a few anxious moments after landing at Dubai in 1973. The ground temperature was right up there; and after the long cold soak at high altitude, the canopies refused to open. The cockpit temperature was rising rapidly, and we were ahead of that curve due to the flying equipment that we wore, not to mention the fatigue after the flight. We were just about to call for outside assistance in getting the canopies open when they decided to cooperate and opened.

During the 1970s, there was a requirement to fly non-stop from the United Kingdom to Singapore, and I was delighted that our sister squadron at Coningsby, 54 Squadron, was tasked with accomplishing that mission. Fourteen plus hours on an ejection seat didn't sound like a lot of fun! These major deployments gave me my first exposure to jetlag, but the flying was satisfying and Singapore was such a different world from the United Kingdom. During our time there we flew low level training missions over the Malaysian jungle, and it was during these missions that the limitations of the Phantom air conditioning system showed themselves.

The Phantom was originally designed as a clean wing interceptor/ combat aircraft to operate at medium to high altitude, and its systems were intended for that environment. The air conditioning system was not intended to operate under conditions of high temperature and high humidity. The consequence of this was that crews had to keep the cockpit temperature selection higher than they wanted so that the entire cockpit wouldn't fill with fog! This unfortunate set of circumstances made the low level missions even more physically demanding, and I'm sure that I lost weight every flight, weight that I could not afford to lose.

———◁◦▷———

An unexpected challenge and pleasure presented itself on 12 April 1972 when I was rostered to fly from Singapore to Hong Kong as the wingman for the squadron boss. The flying into Hong Kong of a pair of Phantoms was largely for symbolic, political reasons—but who was I to question that? The flight time was nearly three and a half hours, so we had one of our friendly Victor aircraft come with us. On arrival into Hong Kong, the Victor circled in the overhead in case there was a problem. In that event, the Phantom would plug in to get some fuel and proceed to divert to Manila in the Philippines.

This was my first of many looks at the famous runway 13 at the old Hong Kong airport of Kai Tak, although I didn't know it at the time. Before being allowed to land a Phantom in Hong Kong, all the involved crews had to witness a landing being carried out from the flight deck of a Hercules transport aircraft. Looking over the captain's shoulder as he came round the famous corner was quite an experience, and I looked forward to doing it in the Phantom.

If you have never been to Hong Kong before the new airport was built, the old Kai Tak airport was located literally next door to Kowloon, one of the most densely populated districts in the world. The airport had a single runway, and takeoffs to the northwest involved following a flight path that went right over downtown Kowloon. Fortunately in the history of the airport, an aircraft never crashed after taking off on runway 31; in such an event, the loss of life would have been unimaginable. Not unnaturally Air Traffic Control preferred to use runway 13 for all departures if at all possible, even to the point of accepting a degree of tailwind.

There was also a daily curfew at the airport which started at midnight so that the locals could get at least some sleep, although Hong Kong was, and no doubt still is, a city that never seemed to sleep. There were other aspects to landing on runway 13. Because the final approach was over a flyover, the actual runway threshold was displaced some distance in to ensure adequate obstacle clearance. There was a complication, however, with the Phantom as we relied quite heavily on our brake parachute for initial deceleration. It was not unknown for the brake chute to fail to deploy and fall onto the runway as a bundle. We then relied on our brakes which were not the most efficient of aircraft brakes.

In order to give us a bit more comfort distance to cover this eventuality, we were authorised to touch down before the marked runway threshold. This, of course, meant that we were coming around the famous corner even lower than was normal for the airliners. That was one approach that I will never forget! I was working quite hard up front as we flew around the corner, but my navigator, Graham Richardson, gave me a running commentary as we flew by the high rise buildings that characterise Hong Kong.

In the event the landing was uneventful, and I got to savour my first taste of expatriate living in an exotic Asian city, little did I realise at the time that I would be experiencing a lot more of Hong Kong in years to come. The plan was that the Hong Kong experience would be shared as much as possible so the crews that flew the two Phantoms up from Singapore would return in the Hercules, and the crews that were scheduled to fly the Phantoms back to Singapore would fly to Hong Kong in the Hercules. The Hercules arrived into Hong Kong as planned, but unfortunately (!) the aircraft then became unserviceable, so another plan had to be organised for the four of us who had flown the Phantoms. This all resulted in our flying back to Singapore via Bangkok in a Cathay Pacific B707—in business class! Little did I know at the time that I would be having a lot more to do with Cathay Pacific in the years ahead.

——◦——

On 31 January 1974, 6 Squadron celebrated its sixtieth anniversary. The squadron had never been disbanded and was the oldest squadron in the RAF in terms of continuous service. The squadron boss at the time was Wing Commander Danny Lavender, and he managed to arrange for the attendance of King Hussein of Jordan at the celebrations at Coningsby. The squadron had an historical connection with service in Jordan after World War II, and this connection was recognised in October 1950 with the presentation of the Royal Jordanian Standard to the squadron at the royal palace in Amman. At one stage during my tour of duty with 6 Squadron, I was the standard bearer. Although it was not publicly displayed very often, I had the honour of carrying the Jordanian standard during the 60th anniversary celebrations. The security during King Hussein's visit was unimaginable for the era. A whole wing of the Officers' Mess was kept for His Majesty and his party. I can remember security personnel patrolling the corridors of the mess carrying automatic weapons. The dining-in night was indeed a memorable affair, and His Majesty presented the squadron with a beautiful scale silver model of the Phantom.

Chapter 4

GLIDING ALONG

You cannot create experience,
you must undergo it.
—Albert Camus

———◦►———

On the gliding front, on moving to Coningsby I became a member of the Four Counties club, an active RAFGSA club based at RAF Spitalgate near the town of Grantham. There was a very good club spirit and the operation was winch only. I did a lot of instructing at the weekends as well as plenty of solo flying.

Domestically, Maren and I bought a small caravan to stay overnight in so maximum use could be made of the days at the club. It was at this stage that Maren decided that if she couldn't beat me, she had better join me more fully in gliding by learning to fly herself. This she duly did and flew the delightful KA8 solo, regularly getting her one hour of local soaring. Maren was happy to be doing that as she had no interest in flying cross country. There wasn't much private ownership at the club, so the club single seaters were allocated for cross country flying to those who put in most of the work.

My special allocated date for using the club Standard Libelle was Sunday, 18 July 1971. The Libelle was a lovely fibreglass aircraft with a snug cockpit and excellent handling for its day. It was one of three Standard

Class fibreglass gliders that made their first appearances in the late 1960s, the other two being the Standard Cirrus and the ASW15. Before the late '60s, gliders were made from wood and doped fabric or metal. I wasn't at the club the previous day, but I heard that conditions had been excellent and that two pilots Barry Dobson and Don Austin (privately owned Standard Cirrus) had each flown tasks of 500 kilometres. The 500 kilometre task would give me one of the two Diamonds that I still needed (having got the first Diamond badge on the declared 310 kilometre out and return flight from Upavon in 1967).

I hardly got any sleep that Saturday night due to excitement over what the next day might bring. I was determined to be fully ready for the day in good time so I was in the club hangar by 7.30AM preparing the glider. I declared an out and return flight to Yeovil, a distance of some 520 kilometres, and took a launch around 10.30AM. Initially conditions were fine, but as time went by I could see that there was a significant problem ahead. The thermals were being marked by cumulus clouds, but as the clouds grew bigger, the tops were coming up against what is known as a temperature inversion. Normally temperature decreases with increasing altitude, but there can be times when it actually increases over a certain altitude band. The effect of the inversion on the tops of the cumulus clouds is that they spread out and cut off the sunlight from reaching the ground. In turn, this puts a stop to the formation of thermals until the spread out cloud breaks up and the sun can get through again.

This can be a significant problem in the United Kingdom and, on this particular day, I was happy to have the freedom to legally climb inside the last cumulus cloud before the large area of spread out. I got as much height inside the cloud as I could and set off on the compass heading towards my goal. The strategy worked beautifully as I had just enough altitude to cross the large area of spread out cloud and reach the first of the active clouds on the other side without being too low. From then on the flight was fairly uneventful until 60 kilometres out from Spitalgate when spread out cloud was again a problem. This time, however, there was sufficient sun's heating getting through to the ground to produce some very weak lift and, after a lot of slow tiptoeing along, I finally had enough altitude to execute the final glide into Spitalgate. The overall task speed was relatively slow, but the flight established a new United Kingdom Out and Return distance record; I received the two distance trophies that the British Gliding Association awarded annually.

———◦———

The next gliding event was my flying a KA6E in my first National Championships which were the Club Class Nationals at the historic Dunstable site in Bedfordshire. The competition generally went well for me, and I was in the lead at the end of the penultimate day. Then, on the seventh and final day, I really blew it and handed the title to Leigh Hood who had been shadowing me in second place. Nonetheless, my performance had been sufficiently good for me to be invited to fly in an international competition at Dunstable called "Euroglide". This event was sponsored by the broadsheet newspaper, the *Daily Telegraph,* pilots being invited to come over from mainland Europe, the aim being to raise the standard of competition flying in the United Kingdom.

This was an invitation that I should have declined as my sister June was to be married in Ireland during the championships. As my father had died in 1969, I should have been the one to have led my sister down the aisle, but selfish pride and the opportunity to fly in such a prestigious event overruled my heart. I was provided with a Cobra15 glider for the event, a type that I had not flown before. The scheduling was ridiculously tight as I was only able to get one reasonable length flight in the glider from Spitalgate before heading for Dunstable.

The final day of the Club Class Nationals was on 13 August and the first day of Euroglide was on 19 August. The competition was a disaster for me! I didn't feel that I was flying particularly well, and it seemed that the Cobra was better suited to the strong conditions of countries like South Africa than the weak and inconsistent conditions of the United Kingdom. I finished up towards the bottom of the results list and returned to Spitalgate with my tail between my legs.

Having dealt with the disappointment of Euroglide over the winter months, I celebrated the arrival of Spring by setting a UK speed record of 93.6 kph over a 200 kilometre triangular course on 29 April 1973 in a Kestrel19, the highest performing glider that I had flown to date. Just a week later I was setting the daily tasks for the annual Inter-Services Competition at Spitalgate.

My next major competition was my second Euroglide in August 1973, the event being held at Lasham in Hampshire which was the location of the largest gliding centre in the United Kingdom. This time I flew in the Four Counties' Kestrel19. The Kestrel19 was an Open Class glider with flaps and a wingspan of 19 metres, and it was manufactured by Slingsby Sailplanes in Yorkshire, being a variant of the Kestrel17 which was manufactured in Germany. The weather conditions weren't great, but we got eight contest days. I was satisfied to finish second in the Open Class.

In October 1973, I headed north to Aboyne in an attempt to gain my third and final Diamond as I shared the club's Kestrel19 with Bob Lyndon. Aboyne is located on the eastern edge of the Scottish Highlands, close to Balmoral Castle, The Queen's summer residence, and just under 50 kilometres to the west of coastal Aberdeen. It is ideally situated to make use of the regular mountain wave, and I was thrilled to get Diamond height on two of my four flights, the highest point being just over 26,000 feet.

Preparation for high altitude flying is important as cold can be a major problem and, of course, a reliable oxygen system is essential. The temperature aspect was underlined during the two high flights as the first time I flew in continuous sunshine and felt very comfortable; whereas the second flight was conducted under extensive cloud, and I really noticed the difference! I was also satisfied to set another United Kingdom speed record in the Kestrel19 on 19 May 1974, flying a 421 kilometre triangle from Spitalgate at an average speed of 90 kph. The year 1974 was a big year for me as I won my first Nationals flying the Kestrel19 in the Open Class Nationals at Dunstable. The year finished with a significant event when I flew a number of First Day Covers to mark the RAFGSA's 25th anniversary, an event organised by Ian Macfadyen.

———◦———

Gliding was becoming a big part of my life, but not so big that there wasn't room for some romance with my wife. Maren gave birth to our first child, Sonja Karoline, on 3 May 1973 during the practice period for the Inter-Services for which I was task setting. As it was our first child, the labour was quite long, but to be present for the birth of our first child was an unforgettable experience.

In August 1974, Maren and I took Sonja to Ireland, and we left her with my mother and stepfather while we went on a holiday. My mother married Tom Stuart in December 1973, a friend of the family whose wife had died earlier of cancer. Tom was an artist, and he and my mother settled down in a remote location in a hilly region inland from Wexford in the southeast of Ireland. Maren and I went off to explore and enjoy the beautifully scenic district of Kerry in the extreme south-west of the country. That was a memorable holiday, not just because of the beautiful scenery.

One day Maren and I hired a small boat with a Seagull outboard engine and went off the coast to try our hands at some mackerel fishing. As it happened the fishing was good, and we became somewhat engrossed in the excitement of the action. After a while we realised that we had drifted quite a distance from the shoreline and, to make matters considerably worse, the small engine refused to start. Now we were only too aware of the fact that we were drifting away from land at a disturbingly fast rate. Our oars were not going to defeat the current, and we had no means of communication.

It was becoming increasingly difficult to maintain a spirit of optimism, and I wondered at what part of France or even Spain we might end up landing. Then the cavalry arrived in the form of a motor launch, the skipper of which had seen our precarious situation. He threw us a rope and kindly towed us back in to harbour. I tried to make light of it all to

Maren, but in reality it hadn't been a good situation—we were fortunate to get away with it as we did.

———◇———

During the early part of 1974, I got the news that I had hoped not to get, that is that I was to be posted to an Air Defence squadron to be formed at the other end of the hangar. That squadron had been 54 Squadron, a Ground Attack squadron, but it was to be retrained and become 111 Squadron, taking over from the Lightning Squadron of the same number that had been based at RAF Wattisham in Suffolk. I was devastated as I just loved the low level Ground Attack environment, but I subsequently discovered that there was a lot more to Air Defence than I had realised.

As if to emphasise my initial disappointment on being posted to an Air Defence squadron, just after I moved up to the other end of the hangar, the Turkish military decided to invade northern Cyprus. I can remember looking out of my new operations room to see my ex-colleagues running towards fully armed Phantoms to fly out to Cyprus. Fortunately they were never involved with combat operations although I understand that it was a close call. I found out that in the Air Defence role, air-to-air refuelling remained a key part of the operation, but radar intercept work was a new challenge for me. Although this was primarily a navigator directed exercise, both crew members played a full part in the proceedings.

Radar interceptions could be undertaken at any level from genuine high level against a supersonic target all the way down to the lookdown, low level environment. Often it would be a case of executing a radar approach and then transferring to the visual to press home the attack. This profile was particularly demanding but satisfying in the low level overland regime. Hard visual manoeuvring at low level overland tested skill and awareness at a high level. It wasn't just a case of gaining the manoeuvring advantage as the attacking aircraft had to ensure that he was solidly within the firing parameters for the weapons system.

Air Defence squadrons would look to use a variety of opposition aircraft types, and the Buccaneer force never disappointed in terms of supplying effective opposition. The planning, coordination, and execution of a four or more aircraft formation low level mission was particularly demanding for the leader. A four ship formation of Phantoms flying in loose battle formation wending their way through narrow Scottish valleys was pretty exciting flying! We did try to avoid overflying villages and other noise sensitive areas, but the noise footprint must have been pretty dramatic from the ground. Whenever I think about this I am reminded of the car sticker that read "Jet noise—the price of freedom".

One of the more exciting types of flying in the Air Defence role was pure combat flying. Typically a squadron would plan a combat phase and all the aircraft were stripped of their external tanks. As we were only operating with internal fuel, the flights were short with lots of action!

The combat phases would also take a considerable toll on aircraft fatigue, thereby shortening airframe life. As the Phantoms aged, squadrons would impose lower G limits on normal training to save fatigue allowance for planned combat phases. To explain, one G represents normal body weight living. When fighter aircraft commence hard manoeuvring, the G loading increases; the tighter the turn for a given airspeed the greater the applied G load. The normal maximum G loading for the Phantom was six G, but the more modern fighters such as the F16 can go up to nine G. A high G environment is not only demanding on the aircraft, it is also physically demanding for the crew.

Sustained high G loads can result in what is known as "greying out" when there is a tunnelling and even a temporary loss of vision, which is not a good situation for a fighter pilot involved in combat! This effect is caused by the G loading forcing the blood down into the lower half of the body and away from the brain. In order to counter this, crews wore G suits which were like corsets that went around the abdomen and the length of both legs. The internal bladders were connected to an aircraft air supply and, as the G load increased, the bladders inflated which put pressure on the lower parts of the body and minimised the tendency of the blood to pool away from the brain.

It is somewhat easier for the pilot as he is applying the stick force resulting in the G loading; but it is harder for the navigator, and it can be made a lot worse if he happens to have his head down looking at the radar screen at the instant a high G loading is applied! The result can be that he is unable to get his head back up if the high G is maintained with resulting impaired crew visual lookout. Pilots would, of course, try to give their navigators some warning of the impending onset of high G, but that wasn't always possible, such as in the case of a late visual acquisition of an enemy in a threatening position requiring a rapid manoeuvring response.

It's difficult to convey what participating in a combat environment is like to somebody who has never had any exposure to it. In spite of some flaws in its portrayal, the movie *Top Gun* does an excellent job in giving some understanding of the speed of events when fighter aircraft get into the combat arena. The movie is not always true to reality, and it should be understood that in the visual combat environment crews need to be constantly ready for a firing opportunity which is invariably brief.

As fighter aircraft became more and more sophisticated over the years, the thought developed that classic air-to-air combat flying would be a thing of the past. This proved not to be the case! The Phantom was not the greatest of fighter aircraft in the area of turning capabilities, so if the enemy could be shot down at long range by a radar missile that would be ideal. However, that brought up the issue of confirming that the radar return was indeed definitely an enemy aircraft; throughout history, aircraft have been shot down by friendly fire. So, in the event of uncertainty, a visual identification had to be carried out, and that brought the attacking aircraft into the visual manoeuvring arena.

When fighter aircraft entered the era of air-to-air missile engagement, a further line of thought developed that the gun would be rendered redundant. This also proved not to be the case! Missiles can misfire, crews can fire them when not solidly within parameters, and the gun proved to remain a very valuable asset, particularly when drawn into close combat manoeuvring. Whatever the type of flying, it was important to develop a high level of crew coordination and understanding which is why the constituted crew concept was favoured. Nonetheless, squadron operating procedures were standardised, and any navigator could be crewed up with any pilot on the squadron and be an effective combination.

The 9th of August 1974 was a black day for RAF Coningsby as the station commander and one of the squadron navigators were killed in a low level midair collision with a Pawnee crop spraying aircraft which was operating in Norfolk, the pilot of the Pawnee also being killed. Neither crew knew about the presence of the other and, as the pilot of the Pawnee pulled up at the end of a spraying run, the aircraft collided. Sadly there was insufficient time to see and avoid each other. At least some good came out of the tragedy in that it brought about a greater degree of coordination between the military and crop spraying operators with regard to the location and timing of their operations.

The powers that be decided that 111 Squadron should move to be based at RAF Leuchars which was near to Dundee and St Andrews in the southeast corner of Scotland; this happened in late 1975. I recall taking off from Coningsby with low cloud and some drizzle, conducting a mission over the North Sea and then pointing the nose towards Scotland to land at Leuchars where there were only broken clouds with superb visibility—*I could get to like this!*

Leuchars offered a couple of distinct operational advantages: firstly, the wonderful Scottish low flying areas were right on the doorstep; and secondly, the Quick Readiness Alert duty was a lot more interesting. I should explain that there were two RAF Phantom squadrons based at Leuchars, 43 Squadron and 111 Squadron. A navy Phantom squadron, 892 Squadron, was also based at Leuchars when they were not away at sea doing carrier operations. The two RAF squadrons shared the 24/7 commitment to have two fully armed aircraft on alert status throughout the year, the purpose being the protection of United Kingdom airspace.

Quick Readiness Alert duties were also fulfilled at Coningsby, but most of the action took place to the far north. The four aircrew and supporting ground crew were housed in a dedicated hangar complex which was positioned close to the runway. The second aircraft was a backup in case of a problem with the primary aircraft. The readiness requirement was RS10 which meant that at any time day or night the primary aircraft was required to get airborne within ten minutes from the alert hooter sounding—or serious questions would be asked!

Sometimes the crew would be brought to RS5 which meant that the crews were fully strapped in and they had to then get airborne within five minutes of the hooter going off. As can be imagined, a no-prior-notice scramble ordered in the middle of the night could be quite an adrenalin-pumping exercise, going from being asleep to being airborne within ten minutes. In reality, there was usually enough intelligence information to bring the crews up slowly to the point of actually getting airborne to intercept the unknown aircraft.

The main "trade" was the Russian long range aircraft codenamed "Bear" which made their way down off the west coast of Norway and to the south of Iceland. From there they would track to the north and west of Scotland as they routed down to their African base. As intercepts frequently took place to the south of Iceland, crews had to wear appropriate protective clothing to be able to survive an ejection into distinctly chilly waters. This took the form of a one piece "bunny" suit which had a one inch thick interior lining of acrylan pile and a long zip which went diagonally across the chest. On top of the bunny suit we wore an immersion suit that was fully waterproof and had rubber seals for the ankles, wrists and neck.

Whilst this entire combination was well suited to its purpose of enhancing survival prospects in cold seawater, life became somewhat warm indoors while waiting for the action. So a typical middle ground state of dress at night was for both the immersion and bunny suits to be unzipped to the waist and flying boots off in order to try and get some precious sleep. You can imagine the scene in the event of a no-notice scramble in the middle of the night!

Operating such a long way north required air-to-air refuelling support, and with a slow build up to actually getting airborne it was possible for the authorities to coordinate the fighter and tanker movements. If there was little or no notice, the fighter just had to get airborne with the tanker following as quickly as possible. There was a problem in this regard as the tanker aircraft were based down south and had a longer distance to transit. If the interception took place with little delay, fighter fuel was usually sufficient to fulfil the mission and return to base. In the event of there being a delay requiring the fighter to take up a holding pattern, it would sometimes be the case that the Phantom didn't have sufficient fuel to wait for and intercept the "trade" and so would have to return to base.

On most occasions it all worked out well and the fighter would get his needed fuel in good time to be ready for the intercept. The Americans had E3a Sentry Airborne Warning and Control System (AWACS) aircraft based in Iceland. These were modified B707 aircraft with a superb on-board radar system, and they often assisted us to execute the interception.

The reaction of the Russian crews varied considerably when intercepted. Some were quite friendly, and there was a famous picture in the *Daily Telegraph* newspaper that showed a Russian crew member at his station in the tail of the Bear giving a thumbs up and holding up a bottle of Coke. Others most definitely didn't welcome our presence. When fully loaded with external fuel tanks and missiles, the Phantom's handling at low speed left a lot to be desired and the Russians knew this. I have been in close formation with a Bear when the captain decided to slow the aircraft right down, at the same time turning towards me and initiating a descent through thick cloud all the way down to low level over the sea.

The intelligence people always wanted to have the individual aircraft identification number, and this necessitated coming up from underneath to a close position in order to read the number. The Russian crew members knew exactly how close we needed to get in order to read the number and at night, just before we reached that position, they would suddenly switch on a very powerful spotlight and aim it at our cockpits. All the Phantom pilot could do was close his eyes and descend rapidly away in order to slowly regain his night vision.

A lot of coordination and control went into the successful execution of Quick Readiness Alert missions, and they were professionally satisfying. I also had the privilege of observing the most spectacularly beautiful displays of Aurora Borealis or Northern Lights when operating so far north.

A particular event that took place during one of my Quick Readiness Alert duties was memorable for all the wrong reasons. I was on a weekend 24-hour spell of duty, and during the day I was just relaxing and enjoying the beautiful weather when I heard a Phantom start up and taxi out for takeoff. It was a naval Phantom as 892 Squadron were on shore at the time. The Phantom took off and went out over the sea before running back in over the airfield at high speed low level; ok, I looked forward to watching the flying display practice.

Having passed the airfield, the pilot pulled the nose up and turned off runway centreline with the throttles to idle to reduce speed, the intention being to carry out a slow flyby with everything hanging down. The orientation of the Quick Readiness Alert complex was such that the Phantom disappeared from my view, and I just waited for it to reappear. After some delay, I heard two Spey engines winding up to full power and then a note change as full reheat was selected. At that instant, the aircraft came into view nose-up and with some bank still on to regain runway centreline. The Phantom continued to descend in a stalled condition and impacted the ground, the point of impact being sufficiently close for me to feel the heat of the explosion. A huge ball of dark smoke went up, and a rescue helicopter was quickly on the scene.

Although I hadn't seen it, I later learned that the impact with the ground had somehow fired the pilot's ejection seat and he survived the accident, although his navigator was tragically killed. The whole thing had been caused by pilot error; it must have been so very hard for the pilot to live with the memory of it all. Even if he was in a wheelchair, he was alive. I later reflected on how lucky I and all the Quick Readiness Alert crew personnel had been; if that fatal final turn had stopped some 30 degrees sooner, none of us would be around to recall what happened.

Ejection seats have been around for a long time, but they have been improved greatly over the years. The earlier seats were fired by a gun, and back injuries were the normal consequence; moreover, there were quite restrictive minimum altitudes and speeds for a safe ejection. Later ejection seats are fired by a series of rocket firings that are milliseconds apart, thus the acceleration is progressive and, as a result, back injuries became a thing of the past. Additionally, the operating envelope became a lot more user friendly, two examples being that an ejection initiated from a stationary position on the ground and being fully inverted at 600 feet would both be successful.

During my time at RAF Leuchars, there was an incident where the crew were very thankful for the capabilities of the modern ejection seat. The leader of a pair of Phantoms had briefed that he would lead his wingman down a night instrument approach and on short finals he would overshoot, the wingman to look ahead and land. The wingman ended up being somewhat stretched back in his formation position, and when the leader initiated his overshoot, the wake from his wings hit the wingman's aircraft causing him to roll uncontrollably to the right. Both crew members managed to initiate successful ejections from very low altitude.

Another memorable incident during my tour on 43 Squadron occurred one evening during an exercise when I had gone home after my spell on duty. I was just going to bed when I heard an unmistakable noise, that of a missile being fired! I rang the squadron and I was advised that a Sidewinder had indeed launched itself, the reason subsequently being traced to some stray volts. It was standard procedure for armed aircraft to be parked with their noses pointed in a safe direction to cover the possibility of such an incident occurring, and in this case the missile proceeded across to the southern side of the airfield without causing any injury or damage.

A 111 Squadron Phantom
with full complement of
missiles and gun pod.

A 111 Squadron
Phantom
intercepting
a Russian Bear
long range aircraft.

Chapter 5

ALLIANCES

Gold medals aren't really made of gold.
They're made of sweat, determination
and a hard-to-find alloy called guts.
—Dan Gable

———◦———

Air Defence squadrons were often involved in major maritime exercises and, as these were often conducted a long distance from the mainland, air-to-air refuelling played a major role. Sometimes the best-laid plans go wrong, and I recall being part of an exercise that was being played out a long way north of Scotland. The planned air-to-air refuelling support hadn't arrived, and I was starting to get tight on fuel. I advised the American controller on one of the ships of the situation, and he calmly responded, "No problem, I'll send you up a Texaco!"

The weather conditions were good, and as I looked down at the ship, I could see that he was true to his word when I saw an A6 tanker aircraft getting airborne and spiralling his way up to my level for the rendezvous. This was going to be a first as I had never taken on fuel from any other type of aircraft than the Victor. In fact it was a lot easier than receiving from a Victor as the A6 crew deployed a centreline hose and proceeded to invite me to take fuel whilst flying at a speed that was much more fighter friendly than that of the Victor—the Trans Atlantic alliance was alive and well!

Another type of aircraft that we worked with regularly was the venerable Shackleton. The Shackleton was developed from the Lincoln bomber which in turn was a derivative of the mighty Lancaster bomber of World War II fame. It was used in maritime patrol and anti-submarine duties, and later was modified for use in Search and Rescue (SAR) and Airborne Early Warning (AEW) duties. Although their cruise speed was slow and their equipment was nowhere near as sophisticated as the American AWACS aircraft, nonetheless, they provided the fighter force with valuable early warning information.

I once positioned between bases on a Shackleton, and I got a taste of the maritime crew's work environment. At one stage in the cruise I was invited to sit in the right hand seat in the cockpit and was given the controls for a while. I had never flown a heavy aircraft before, but I just couldn't believe the physical force required to manoeuvre the Shackleton. Having had a go, I returned to the rear giving thanks that I flew Phantoms for a living!

During the early part of my time at Leuchars I had the opportunity to fire my first live air-to-air missile. What a thrill it was to feel the Sidewinder thunder away from its rail on the Phantom and to watch it as it flew and made minor tracking adjustments before impacting with the target—success!

—◦—

Another big year for my gliding was 1975. It started in May with my flying the Four Counties' Kestrel19 in the Open Class Nationals at Husbands Bosworth in central England. I came in second on the first competition day and then proceeded to become last the following day by being too aggressive and landing out just after the first turning point! A couple of daily first placings pulled me up to my final position of fifth, but my overall performance over the previous few years had ensured me a place in the British team for the World Championships to be held in Finland in 1976.

World Championships are normally held every two years with a so-called Pre-Worlds being held in the intervening year. These Pre-Worlds were important events as they afforded pilots, crews and members of the hosting organisation a valuable opportunity to get the whole operation in good working order. They also gave pilots good exposure to the weather patterns that they might expect the following year, as well as the terrain, landing out prospects, available accommodation, local food options, and a host of other important points. I always believed that going to the Pre-Worlds was most important, and there was a nice feeling of familiarity on arrival back the next year for the big event. Accordingly, my Open Class teammate Bernie Fitchett and I travelled over to Rayskala in June 1975 for the Pre-Worlds. Bernie flew his ASW17 and I flew the Four Counties' Kestrel19.

Maren and I had recently purchased our first brand-new car, an Eastern Block Moskvitch which cost the princely sum of £2,500 (almost $4,000 today). There is a degree of truth in the saying that, "You get what you pay for"—both the build quality and the reliability of the Moskvitch did leave something to be desired. The Finns had a good laugh on our arrival as they called the Moskvitch, "The fastest tractor in the West". They also commented on the huge disparity between the financial worth of the vehicle and the contents of the trailer!

My crew comprised Maren and my regular crew chief Albert Johnson. Albert had crewed for me for a number of competitions and we had developed a good working relationship. A good crew is extremely important in a high level competition. A single crew person is sufficient for the smaller gliders, but two crew members are really needed to provide support for the bigger Open Class gliders. In the event of there being two crew persons, one has to be designated as the crew chief to cover situations where there may be a difference of opinion. Although some technical knowledge is a bonus, there are no particular requirements for somebody to be a crew member—common sense, reliability, and a high level of motivation being the most desirable attributes.

Crew duties can vary, and it is important for pilot and crew to get together and talk through how the team is going to operate as pilots approach things differently. I liked to leave the daily management of the glider to my crew so that I could concentrate on the operational aspects. Albert had a good all round basic technical knowledge, he was always well organised, he was 100 percent reliable, and he took a keen interest in the flying side. He knew my routine and what I wanted, but he also knew that he could use his initiative, for example, in deciding to connect the trailer and head up the last leg of the task when there were indications that the weather wasn't as good as expected. Taking such action could result in saving time in the event of an outlanding and subsequent retrieve.

For the Pre-Worlds in Finland, Maren had not crewed for me before, but she supported Albert well and managed the domestic scene with her usual flair. Maren has supported me at all the major competitions that I have flown in, even though she only formally crewed for me once. I have been so thankful for her support and for being able to share the highs and lows over the years. The three of us slept in tents for the event and that worked out well. Many of the nations and their top pilots were not present in 1975, and the Open Class only had a small number of competitors.

The soaring conditions in 1975 were excellent, and I recall walking over to the briefing hangar one morning at around 8.45AM and observing an intermittent flash to the south over the trees. I later found out that it was the famous German record-breaking pilot Hans Werner Grosse as he was gliding out to find his first thermal of the day in a successful attempt to fly the first 1,000 kilometre triangle in Europe.

———◦———

This was my first gliding outside of the United Kingdom, and there were certain striking differences. The visibility was generally excellent in comparison to the UK, and the first time I became airborne, I was astonished to find that I could see both of the turnpoints of my 300 kilometre triangle. The next thing that impressed itself upon me was that there seemed to be nothing but trees and lakes everywhere. I quickly found out that was not the case as there were plenty of suitable fields for outlandings except in certain areas, one being close in to Rayskala. When pilots finished their tasks coming in from the northwest, there were only trees and water for the last 10 kilometres. A decision had to be made as to whether a pilot had enough altitude to safely make it home or whether he had to turn back to make a safe outlanding. There were some interesting final glides in 1975, including one Italian pilot not making it and having to land in the lake just before the airfield, breaking the fuselage of his Standard Cirrus in the process.

Another thing that impressed me about Finland was the seemingly impenetrable language which seemed to be related to no other European language, except for Hungarian. I quickly found out that the best chance of being understood was to make contact with a younger person, although the organisation had issued explanatory notes in Finnish to hand to people after an outlanding.

The flying generally went well, my main competition being Bernie Fitchett, my teammate. There was one interesting flight where the organisation had set us a distance task in relatively poor conditions and we ended up flying a greater distance than expected. The late landing was followed by a late retrieve that lasted well into the early hours of the morning. I was pleased to end up winning the competition, although I was conscious of the fact that all the big names were not present.

The other big gliding event in 1975 was my competing in the Kestrel 19 in another Euroglide competition at Dunstable. After a seven day contest, I ended up second in the Open Class, but there was an additional bonus on Day 2 when we were set a 350 kilometre out and return task towards Wales. As we were on the grid waiting for take-off, the conditions didn't look too encouraging, and I was aware that most pilots were dumping their water ballast in order to optimise their climbing performance in the anticipated weak conditions.

High performance gliders are equipped with water tanks or bags in the wings so that the overall weight can be increased up to the maximum certified limit. Under strong lift conditions, gliders should be flown at high cruising speeds; and if they are near maximum weight, the resulting glide angle is flatter than if they are light. For a given airspeed, the heavier glider will cover a greater distance from a given altitude. A further benefit is that when the heavier glider pulls up in strong lift, there will be a greater gain in altitude over the lighter glider. The water can, of course, be jettisoned during flight if the conditions become weak. The downside of carrying the extra weight in flight is that the circling speed has to be increased as the stall speed has increased; but overall, depending on the type of glider, the advantages outweigh the disadvantages when flying in moderate to strong conditions.

Back to the grid at Dunstable, I decided to keep my water on board as I could always dump it locally before start if the conditions were as weak as they appeared to be. Having been towed up and soaring locally waiting for the start gate to open, I became aware that the conditions appeared to be improving. The end of the day saw my setting a new United Kingdom speed record for a 300 kilometre out and return task with a speed of 106 kph—I was very glad that I had kept my water on board!

———◦———

That was the last of my four United Kingdom records. National local records come within the reach of many pilots, but national overseas records and particularly world records are increasingly becoming a possibility only for those with plenty of time and money. Many world records are now being flown to the lee of the Andes in Argentina.

Thermals are rising columns of warm air within which glider pilots circle tightly to gain altitude. Glider pilots also use wave lift which utilises the secondary effects of hill lift that can produce a mirror image process in the higher levels. Unlike when using thermals, pilots flying under good wave conditions are able to keep the wings of the glider level for extended periods of time and are therefore able to maintain a good speed over the ground. Moreover, pilots are typically flying at considerably greater altitudes when using wave than when using thermals. Because the air is thinner at high altitudes, for a given indicated airspeed, the speed over the ground is significantly greater than for the same airspeed at typical thermalling altitudes.

To give some idea of the performance that gliders are capable of achieving, the world maximum free distance record stands at 3,009 kilometres, the world record speed over a 300 kilometres triangular course is 225 kph and the world absolute height record stands at 15,460 metres, or 50,721 feet—way above the normal maximum altitude of airliners.

Finally, November 1975 saw me starting my gliding with the Portmoak club, a civilian club located on the shore of Loch Leven in between two hills about a half hour's drive from Leuchars. Portmoak was a large club that offered both winch and aerotow launches. The flying was very different from what I had been used to. A lot of the soaring was done using hill or ridge lift when the glider soars in the rising air as it is forced over the hill when a wind is blowing. When conditions were right for wave soaring, pilots could either be towed directly into the lift or it was sometimes possible to transition from ridge lift into the wave.

Of course what I had been most used to was soaring and flying cross country using thermals, and Scotland is not renowned for its thermal soaring, although there can be the occasional good day. Additionally, flying cross country using thermals can give problems as there are many areas where there is a distinct shortage of decent outlanding possibilities. I did a lot of instructing during my time with the Portmoak club, and during the winter months there were many days when I was very glad to have the use of my bunny suit under my flying suit! Although the temperatures were often on the cold side of chilly, the warmth of the club spirit more than compensated.

The downside of flying from Portmoak was that I was unable to keep in practice with performance cross country flying and the World Championships in 1976 kept getting closer. On the other side of the coin, I was hungry for my cross country flying!

April 1976 saw me down at Bicester and having my first flight in a brand-new ASW17, the RAFGSA flagship that I would be flying in Finland later in the year. Team meetings were held periodically to discuss logistics and strategy. The team manager was Roger Barrett and he did an excellent job. I remember one particular meeting when Roger wrote on the whiteboard, "What's so special about George Moffat?" George Moffat was the top American Open Class pilot who had won his second World Championship in Australia in 1974; we had a good discussion!

One of the perennial problems with participation in World Championships has been obtaining sponsorship. As in previous years, a great deal of time and effort was expended in trying to get a suitable sponsor without success, but finally we managed to gain the support of the United Kingdom division of SAAB, the Swedish car manufacturer. Each of the four pilots and crews were supplied with a new SAAB 99 automobile fitted with a towbar, and the team did its part by displaying large endorsement stickers on the sides of the glider cockpits, the car doors and along the sides of the trailers.

Although there wasn't a great deal of room in the cockpit of the ASW17, I fell in love with the glider from the outset. The handling was truly delightful for a glider of 20.5 metres wingspan and it had superb stability. Open Class gliders are always going to present challenges on the ground and the ASW17 was no exception. The main wing panels each weighed in at around 100kg and rigging was not done in five minutes, hence the advisability of having the second crew member. Albert and I did have another challenge as the money box had been emptied in purchasing the glider and there was no money left to buy a new trailer. I was advised that we would just have to set about modifying the old wooden Kestrel trailer to accommodate the ASW17. Albert and I duly embarked on the project at Syerston, an RAF airfield near Newark in Nottinghamshire where both the main Air Cadet gliding school and the Four Counties Club were located, the club having moved from Spitalgate. After a lot of hard work, we professed ourselves satisfied with the end result.

Later in the year we were on our way down to Lasham in Hampshire to compete in the Open Class Nationals as a warm up before going to the 15th World Gliding Championships in Finland. There was some high drama before the first day of the Nationals when I was called over the public address system to take a phone call. Being a club aircraft, the ASW17 had been flown by somebody else for a different competition, and the pilot and his crew had been on their way down to Lasham when a big truck overtook the combination. The ensuing oscillations of the trailer were amplified by misjudged inputs from the driver, and it all ended up with the trailer on its side at the edge of the motorway. On hearing this news, my heart headed towards my mouth as not only was I just about to compete in the Open Class Nationals but my crew and I were scheduled to travel to Finland for the World Championships in just over two weeks time.

Albert and I jumped into our crew car and headed up to the location of the incident. When I got out of the car and saw the trailer on its side, my heart sank, but the heavy feeling was replaced by great relief after I gingerly opened the trailer door, peered inside and realised that the glider was undamaged. All the hard work that Albert and I had put in on the trailer fittings had paid off!

As for the Nationals, I finished second after seven competition days. Before the British team set off for Finland, we were all invited to meet Prince Phillip as he was the patron of the British Gliding Association. I often wondered later what the executives of the various organisations that had been approached for sponsorship would have thought when they saw the press coverage of the British Gliding Team driving in to the front grounds of Buckingham Palace with SAAB stickers clearly showing everywhere.

———— ‹o› ————

As my crew and I headed for Finland, Maren headed for Norway in an advanced state of pregnancy to see her family. Nine days after the end of the Nationals, I got airborne from Rayskala for my first flight of the practice week. World Championships are preceded by an official practice week, and it offers a good opportunity for a final shakedown and proving of equipment and procedures.

It was during this week that life became interesting for me. Everything was good with the glider and equipment, and I had an experienced crew in Albert and Jock Wishart. I was happy with my domestic arrangements as I had set up my tent over the other side of the airfield right away from all noise and general disturbance. The problem lay with my psychological state. The big name pilots from around the world, none of whom had been present the previous year for the Pre-Worlds, were now all here. Pilots like Klaus Holighaus from Germany who owned one of the main glider factories in that country and who was also a brilliant glider designer. Dick Johnson was a legendary American pilot who was famous for his flight test reporting. There was also Dick Butler, a top American Open Class pilot who flew his Glasflugel 604 very well. These were pilots I had only read about before, and now I was about to compete against them.

The result of all this negativity was that I tried too hard during the practice week and ended up getting low and only finding weak lift, all the time thinking that I was not good enough and that I didn't deserve to be flying in the World Championships. In retrospect, there was no doubt that I was in a downward mental spiral and that things were getting worse. Fortunately my team manager, Roger Barrett, realised what was happening to me, and he called me aside one day to have a private chat. He didn't use many words, and I shall never forget what he said, "Relax George, fly the way you've always flown". That was sufficient to open my mental dump valve and the corner was turned!

The Championships didn't start too auspiciously as I came 13th on the first day. I pulled back my confidence the next day which I won, pulling me up to 6th overall. The third day was one of high drama! I set off on the briefed distance task only to land out some 50 kilometres away with a major problem involving water and instruments—it was that sort of day. The rules in force then allowed a retrieve back to the airfield and a subsequent takeoff to have another go. My crew found me, we de-rigged the glider and broke every Finnish speed limit getting back to the airfield as quickly as we could.

When we arrived, the whole ground component of the British Team was there waiting for us. I got out of the car and stood well back as my crew, ably supported by other members of the team, set a world record time for the rigging of an ASW17, a glider that is demanding to rig at the best of times. I was thrust into the cockpit with my maps and water, some tape was quickly applied to the wing panel joints, and I was sent on my way for the second time. The whole effort was worth it as I ended up being 8th for the day in my class and 8th overall.

I then won the next day, Day 4, which gave us the best conditions so far, my winning speed over the task distance of 526 kilometres being 112 kph and bringing me up to 2nd overall. Day 5 saw me landing out and coming in 6th for the day, but finding that was good enough to put me into the overall lead. Day 6 was another speed day which I won and increased my overall lead.

I was now looking at the 7th and final day. The weather conditions were not at all good with a possibility of thunderstorms in the local area and very poor visibility. My Open Class teammate Bernie agreed to help me in any way he could to ensure my victory; the only problem being that as I worked hard to maintain altitude pre-start, Bernie was having a bad time down low and was taking a long time to get up to my altitude. Finally I looked at my watch and decided I just had to get going. I advised Bernie and set out into the murk.

The task was a relatively modest 220 kilometre triangle, but the going was dreadfully slow. Then around halfway down the first leg I couldn't believe my eyes as a curtain appeared to be opening up in the distance and I seemed to be seeing some blue sky and sunshine. So it proved to be and, with the sun's power hitting the ground and some regular cumulus clouds around, my morale took a definite upturn.

Suddenly I had the feeling that I was no longer alone. I scanned around and I just couldn't believe what I was seeing. Not far off my left wingtip there was a German registered motorglider in formation with me at the same altitude, and I could see somebody in the right hand seat holding what appeared to be a TV camera as he filmed my every move.

I was not amused! Here I was on the final day of my first World Gliding Championships trying to secure my victory and the papparazzi were in close attendance. I gesticulated as best I could to indicate that I would really quite like to be on my own. After a while the crew either understood my message or they had run out of filming capacity because they turned away and left me to it.

After turning the final point, I started the leg home. I could see ahead that I would be entering the same murky conditions that I had been in before the start. I got lower and lower until I felt some air that held a faint promise of yielding some life, so I gently started to manoeuvre and feel what was going on. At that point I was aware of two other Open Class gliders who were slightly lower than I was and gliding out towards Rayskala. Almost at the same time, I was aware of many Standard Class gliders whose final leg coincided with the Open Class. I stupidly became distracted by all the gliders; there was no usable lift where I was, and I ended up landing in a large field below along with a number of Standard Class gliders. I should, of course, have used my precious height to glide out for maximum distance. I was furious with myself as I waited for my crew and wondered if I had blown my victory.

In due course, my crew arrived and we de-rigged the glider, then drove back to the airfield to await the news. It took awhile for the film assessors to make up their minds, but then it was confirmed; although my lead had been reduced, it wasn't by as much as I had expected, and my victory was confirmed. Great Britain had their first single seat gliding World Champion since the great Philip Wills won in Spain in 1952. My dream to win the World Gliding Championships had come true. The two Open Class Polish pilots, Ziobro and Muszczynski, who had been pairs flying took the second and third positions respectively.

Now the party could begin! My team manager, Roger Barrett, shared with me later that he had felt the strain of that final day so much that he had to get on his bicycle and ride off into the forest. One of the first things I did after my victory was confirmed was to ring Norway and let Maren know the result; in fact I rang her many times during the evening!

Roger kindly agreed to approve the funding of Maren flying from Oslo to Helsinki the next day, and he arranged for a light aircraft to pick her up from there to bring her out to Rayskala.

That was quite a party, and I'm not sure when I finally got to my bed on the other side of the airfield, although I do remember thinking that the night was very short. Dawn was very early in Finland in mid-summer, and the birds got into their full repertoire at a time when one could reasonably expect to be asleep.

The closing ceremony the next day was memorable, made all the more so by Maren's presence, bearing in mind that she was heavily pregnant at the time. I got to meet the legendary Hans Werner Grosse for the first time after the ceremony. Ingo Renner won the Standard Class, and in those days the organisation actually awarded prizes to the class winners as well as the honour of retaining the cup until the next World Championships. I received a colour TV which was much appreciated, but I couldn't believe it when I heard that Ingo was going to receive a brand-new glider! It was to be a PIK20 which was an impressive 15 metre glider that was produced by Eiri Avion in Finland—it was the glider type that he had flown to victory.

—◦—

My first World Championships had been memorable for many reasons, not the least of which had been a remarkable example of international cooperation during the event. On 22 June (the day of my amazing outlanding and relight), Dick Butler outlanded and broke in two the fuselage of the big 604 as well as badly damaging the undercarriage. He rang Richard Schreder, the United States team manager, and gave him the bad news. Richard got to work, and when Dick and his crew brought the damaged glider back, there was a strong band of specialists ready to do battle. The list included Gerhard Waibel (chief designer in Schleichers, one of the two main glider factories in Germany), Klaus Holighaus, Francois Ragot (who was also competing and who was a member of the Concorde design group), Walter Schneider of the LS glider factory in Germany, and finally repair experts from the Eiri Avion factory in Finland.

Dick Butler is renowned for his fighting spirit, and that enthused the international team of experts as they set upon the task. Around midnight Klaus excused himself in order to get some sleep before competing the next day. Work continued all through the night; both the fuselage and tailplane were repaired, and the repairs were given the heat lamp treatment. Finally the undercarriage was expertly repaired by one of the Eiri Avion repair team who welded the undercarriage assembly using only the old tubing. The next morning, as the last Open Class glider rolled down the runway, the hangar doors opened and an airworthy 604 was pushed out. Dick hadn't had much sleep, but he went on to compete that day. The whole operation had been an astonishing display of determination and international cooperation.

And so the victorious journey home to be greeted at the arrival port of Felixstowe by Air Vice-Marshal Brian Stanbridge, chairman of the Royal Air Force Gliding and Soaring Association (RAFGSA), Air Commodore John Brownlow, deputy chairman of the RAFGSA, and various media representatives. In the months that followed my return from Finland, I attended various gliding social events to share about the victory and to hand out trophies, including the British Gliding Association's annual dinner. A particularly memorable event was the RAFGSA's annual prize giving when I was presented with a beautiful painting depicting the ASW17 in flight over Finland. I was expected to make a speech that evening, but I was just too overcome with emotion to say very much.

A proud moment—victory in the 1976
World Gliding Championships
in Finland.

Chapter 6

CROSS COUNTRY CURRENTS

The sky is the limit.
You never have the same experience twice.
—Frank McCourt

———◇———

Ten days after the final competition day at Rayskala, I was back in the Phantom having a dual check after my extended time away. Two weeks later, the Squadron was on its way to Luqa, a military base in Malta for its annual air-to-air gunnery camp. A small number of Canberra aircraft, modified to tow a large banner target, accompanied us for the duration of our detachment. The Canberra was a light bomber that had been used in the nuclear strike role as well as being a tactical bomber and later serving as a photographic and electronic reconnaissance aircraft. It served the Phantom force well, both as a simulated threat for routine air defence training and for towing the banner target for live air-to-air gunnery.

Air-to-air gunnery is an extremely demanding exercise. In actual combat, getting into position to fire takes considerable skill, patience, and determination, any firing opportunity inevitably being brief. For our air-to-air firing over the Mediterranean Sea, the Canberra crew would set up on a racetrack pattern at medium altitude and the Phantom crews would position themselves slightly above and inside the pattern. On the call of the Phantom pilot, the Canberra crew would initiate a gentle left hand turn, and the fighter would commence the attack run closing at a considerable rate. The Phantom navigator would lock the radar onto the radar reflecting bar at the front of the banner and call the range from target as it rapidly reduced.

There was an ideal firing range and the burst from the gun would be around half a second giving the pilot just enough time to pull up and break to the right away from the Canberra and the banner. The achieved angle off of the banner from the Phantom's attack track gave good target exposure as well as ensuring the safety of the Canberra crew as 20mm shells whistled past! Occasionally the angle off would only be just enough, and the Canberra crews could actually hear the bullets go by. The Phantom gunsight was relatively basic which meant that the aircraft needed to be placed smoothly "in the slot" to maximise the chance of success. Pilot skill was paramount, but it was satisfying when success was achieved as there was quite an element of "seaman's eye" required.

On one particular air-to-air gunnery sortie, my navigator Pete Gray and I managed to achieve a score of 92.5 percent which was definitely satisfying! A small number of pilots could be firing on the same banner, and the weapons instructors scored each individual by counting the number of holes in the target that showed witness marks in the colour of the bullets that the gun had been loaded with. So if there had been three pilots firing on the same target, each pilot would have been firing bullets whose tips had been dipped into different colour paint. I don't recall there ever being a situation where two pilots fired on the same target with the same colour bullets! I had enjoyed weaponry very much in the air-to-ground role on 6 Squadron but I found air-to-air gunnery to be every bit as enjoyable and even more demanding.

Just under two months after my dual check I flew a Phantom to RAF Wattisham to meet up with a television team for filming in both the Phantom and the ASW17. After landing back at Leuchars the following day, Air Traffic Control gave me some unusual taxiing instructions, and I was finally marshalled into a position just in front of the old control tower which was the squadron building. As I came to a halt and shut the engines down, a group of my colleagues came out onto the observation balcony holding up a large banner that read, "IT'S A BOY!"

Before I flew over to Wattisham, Maren had been heavily pregnant, but life had to go on, although I was sorry not to have been in attendance for the birth of our son, Brian Edward. Brian decided that he wasn't going to take any nutrition after birth, so he was placed in an incubator for a while, after which he cooperated and gained weight normally.

A routine sequence of squadron flying followed during the months after Brian's birth until early March 1977 when I took the editor of a local St Andrew's newspaper, Malcolm Campbell, on a flight mission. Malcolm was a special member of the Officers' Mess at Leuchars, and he was a great supporter of the station and its activities. For the mission, I was to be one of a pair, the leader being Squadron Leader Dick Northcote. The mission profile comprised two supersonic runs over the North Sea at high altitude, each aircraft taking it in turn to be the enemy target, also meeting up with a Victor tanker for some much needed fuel. The flight went pretty much as planned and Malcolm even managed to get the radar locked on when we were the attacking aircraft. It was a demanding mission for a first flight in a fast jet that lasted just over two hours; and although Malcolm had to make use of the sick bag during the flight, he thoroughly enjoyed the experience and subsequently wrote an excellent article in his paper.

—◦—

The next major gliding event for me was when I was invited to participate in an annual invitation event that was sponsored by Smirnoff of vodka fame. It was called the Smirnoff Derby and involved flying across the whole of the United States of America from west to east. The event took place in May 1977, and it was the third derby to be flown. There were only five pilots competing in the 1977 event, George Moffat, Wally Scott, and Al Leffler being the American pilots, Ingo Renner from Australia, and myself, three of us being current or ex-world champions.

This was the most exciting event that I have participated in outside of World Championships flying. The journey from Scotland to California seemed to take forever, and I was utterly exhausted by the time I reached my motel room, but touched to see the flowers and bowl of fruit that the local gliding club had kindly put in my room. Arrangements had been made for me to fly a Pik20b belonging to the Seaborn family; it was good to meet such great people on their Californian ranch. The family owned a large recreational vehicle that they graciously made available for the event.

The whole event was going to be a major challenge for the crew, every bit as much as for the pilot. I felt well-supported as the Seaborn family would also have the services of my regular crew chief Albert who had also flown over from the United Kingdom to be part of the experience. Hannes Linke was the director of the Derby, and he had two towplanes at his disposal in case one had a problem.

I managed to get four practice flights out of El Mirage, a famous gliding site located in the desert interior before heading off to another motel room in Los Angeles. I was so excited about the prospect of what was to start the next day that I got almost no sleep that night! The next morning we all gathered at one of the Los Angeles general aviation airports for the extensive media coverage that preceded our departure and routing over the San Gabriel mountains into the Mojave Desert. We used five towplanes for the departure so that we could rendezvous in good time for the official start of the first race which was to an airport in Phoenix, Arizona.

Each start would be a "racehorse" start; that is, we would all get together at the same location and adjust our individual altitudes so that we were all at the same height in a wide circle. When the designated leader was happy that all was good, he gave a countdown to the start. At that point the race was on and we rolled wings level and headed out on course.

In competition flying, some pilots like to closely follow other better pilots to gain an advantage over many of the competitors, the practice being called "leeching", but for this event it was definitely not a problem. Each of us was an experienced pilot, and we each had our own ideas as to how to fly the task! You should remember that this was pre-GPS flying, so we had to navigate using a map and compass. I had never flown cross country in the United States before, and I found the navigation challenging, especially during the first leg where navigational features were few and far between.

At one point I was at a relatively low altitude over pretty featureless terrain in only weak lift and wondering why I had put my hand up for the event! From Phoenix we routed via Las Cruces in New Mexico, Odessa and then Dallas in Texas, Oklahoma, Springfield and St Louis in Missouri, Chicago in Illinois, Columbus in Ohio, and Latrobe in Pennsylvania—the final goal being Frederick in Maryland. I finished the event in the silver medal position behind Ingo Renner. The next day, for the benefit of the media, we were assisted by extra towplanes to carry out a stream arrival, descent, and landing on the short takeoff and landing (STOL) runway at Dulles International Airport near Washington, DC.

The Smirnoff Derby was over for another year, and it was such an outstanding experience. Every day produced fresh navigational challenges and differing types of terrain. It was of course a team effort, and I was very grateful for the Seaborn family's support in so many ways, not the least being the use of the family glider. It was hard work for the crews in view of the great distances that were covered over the total eleven days, but at least they got to see different scenery each day.

I was very impressed to see that George Moffat's wife, Suzanne, was his only crew member—a remarkable lady! As George had been heard to comment, "Suzanne may not know how to fix a fuel pump, but she can sure find someone who can." Every evening a social event had been organised at a local glider pilot's house, and the media coverage and public interest in the event was truly amazing. In view of that, it was astonishing to me that Smirnoff only sponsored two more of these outstanding events; I was just so thankful to have been part of one of them.

I have so many memories of the event, but three come to mind particularly, the first being a flight with George Moffat on a rest day in a Great Lakes biplane trainer that dated from the early 1930s. The second great memory was final gliding into Las Cruces late in the day. Although dusk was rapidly approaching, lift was still available from the semi-desert terrain; indeed lift can sometimes continue after dark after a very hot day so the glider pilot must take care to land before it is officially dark. The final glide into Las Cruces was memorable because the street and building lights of the town were coming on, and the sight of the majestic Organ Mountains some ten miles or sixteen kilometres to the east of the town was truly impressive. The final significant memory of the Smirnoff Derby was on one day when, as usual, we all started at the same time. I never saw another glider all day, but I finished within ten seconds of Ingo Renner—that was memorable!

The final major gliding event of the year was the Open Class Nationals at Husbands Bosworth in Leicestershire, and I flew the familiar ASW17 into second place. I was honoured in December 1977 to be awarded the Royal Aero Club's Gold Medal by Prince Charles. The RAEC's Gold medal is awarded for outstanding achievement in aviation, and it was humbling to reflect on some of the previous recipients, the Wright brothers, Louis Bleriot, Alcock and Brown, and United States astronauts Armstrong, Aldrin and Collins.

My humbled state continued when I was advised that I was to be awarded the Member of the Order of the British Empire (MBE) in the New Year's Honours List, made even more special by the fact that it was to be awarded on the Civil List on the recommendation of the Prime Minister. It was awarded for "Services to Gliding", and the award reflected not only my World Championships victory but a number of other contributions to the movement, including the setting up of a training scheme for junior pilots. The scheme paved the way for the eventual inauguration of the highly successful annual Junior Nationals. My mother came over from Ireland and she, Maren, and I went off to Buckingham Palace dressed up in our finest attire. To receive the MBE from The Queen in Buckingham Palace was indeed a special experience.

In June 1977 I was promoted to Squadron Leader and posted to the sister RAF squadron at Leuchars, 43 Squadron, known as "The Fighting Cocks". All of the squadrons that I have had the honour of serving on have had a distinguished history of service in various parts of the world. I served on 43 Squadron as a Flight Commander of one of the two flights, having a number of pilots and navigators under me. Going from being a Flight Lieutenant on 111 Squadron to a Squadron Leader on 43 Squadron was more than just walking across the ramp and laying claim to an office and a personal locker. The workload and responsibilities were much greater, and Maren relates how Sonja used to come home and ask, "Is Daddy asleep or flying?" The flying wasn't much different between the two squadrons so at least that was familiar, although I was now flying a slightly different version of the Phantom.

In November 1977 the squadron got to pit their skills against the American Aggressors. This was a specialist unit that operated the Northrop F5 light fighter aircraft painted in genuine Soviet camouflage markings. Moreover the experienced pilots flew their aircraft and applied their tactics exactly as the Russian pilots would. The F5 was reasonably representative of some of the early Mig fighters, and they proved to be a formidable foe, having an excellent turning performance and being very difficult to acquire visually.

I enjoyed routine squadron flying for the next three years with some challenging opposition in terms of coming against a wide variety of aircraft that included Canberras, Vulcans, Buccaneers, and Jaguars, as well as working with the navy on exercises. The squadron was presented with a particularly challenging target when it was arranged for us to simulate defending the United Kingdom against a high level supersonic threat in the form of the Concorde! Meeting the Quick Readiness Alert (QRA) commitment was also a lot more rewarding than QRA down south in that I got to intercept a significant number of Soviet long range aircraft on a regular basis.

In 1979, the venue for our annual air-to-air gunnery training changed as Dom Mintoff, the Maltese Prime Minister, decided that we were no longer welcome in Malta. So we headed in a more easterly direction and deployed to RAF Akrotiri in Cyprus. The Maltese people had been very friendly to us and so were the Greek Cypriots. Cyprus is, of course, a larger island with more variety in its terrain, and it was possible to be enjoying the beach and, if conditions became too hot, to go skiing on Mount Olympus in the Troodos range of mountains in the southern part of the island on the same day. The weather conditions were usually reliable at the time we were there which made the accomplishment of the goals all the easier.

I have so many fond memories of Cyprus, including fish lunches at Paphos and gliding out of Kingsfield; it was just such a shame that the island ended up being divided after the Turkish invasion of 1974. As usual, the weather conditions were good in May 1979, but it was very hot and I felt some sympathy for the ground crew, especially the armourers, as they worked hard under a blazing sun to service the hot gun pods and reload them in readiness for the next sortie.

I then got the idea that we should do something for the ground crew as a thank-you for all their hard work. I put it to the squadron boss, Ian McBride, that it would be good to put on a bit of a firepower demo for the ground crew and, as it would involve pointing the nose at the sea, it needed somebody who had ground attack experience to do it—hint, hint! To my great surprise, Ian thought it was a good idea and agreed to the proposal. He then had to present the plan to the senior Air Officer at Akrotiri for his approval and to my even greater astonishment he also agreed. So a date was scheduled and early that day a time expired multi-seat emergency rubber dinghy was towed out an appropriate distance from the cliffs overlooking the sea.

Normally during our air-to-air training, because of the closing speed, the gun firing time was only around half a second, but on this occasion I was given approval to fire the gun for a full five seconds! Ken Wood and I took off with a fully loaded gun and departed to the east in readiness for the run in. As we flew in on our run, I was aware of the large number of people at the top of the cliff with their knees dangling over the edge.

We flew in at low level to arrive at our pull up point just in front of the cliff, and I commenced the attacking manoeuvre using maximum reheat, not because I needed the power but to make it more spectacular for the onlookers! I visually acquired the target and used the modified aiming procedure that had been agreed with the squadron weapons instructor, Lloyd Doble. It all worked out exactly as planned, and I was aware of the target being laced with 20mm shells before finally pulling out of the dive and giving the gun a well-earned rest. The crowd was thrilled!

———◦———

In August 1979 I commanded a detachment to Rygge, a Norwegian Air Force base relatively close to Maren's home farm. As well as fighting the Norwegian F5s there was a requirement to fly a single aircraft up to the northern base of Bodo north of the Arctic Circle. I decided to claim this one for myself and, before landing at Bodo, my navigator and I went farther to have a look at our diversion field, Bardufoss. It was fortunate that the weather conditions were good as Bardufoss is located in a deep valley and the published instrument approach procedures were quite interesting!

Anyway, it was a beautiful summer day and having let down and over-flown the airfield, I turned left and pointed the nose towards Bodo. As well as turning left I brought the nose up having selected full cold power as the mountains nearby were pretty imposing. After a short time, I realised that cold power wasn't going to cut the mustard, so it was a matter of top left corner with the throttles and then I could see that we were going to be ok! Fortunately we had the fuel and we descended into Bodo where it was the most perfect summer afternoon. I approached from over the sea for an uneventful landing and taxied in.

When I visually acquired the marshaller who would give the visual signals for final parking, I couldn't believe what I was seeing as he was stripped to the waist and his skin was suntanned to the colour of mahogany—this was north of the Arctic Circle! Norway is a very long country, and Maren told me that when the weather conditions are poor down south, they are usually good up north; at that time conditions down south were indeed relatively poor.

Another lasting memory of the detachment was the social evening that we hosted in the Officers' Mess for our hosts and their wives. We had anticipated this event before leaving Scotland, and we had brought over what seemed like a ridiculously large consignment of good, single malt whiskey. The evening arrived, and we set everything up in the function room in good time. The glasses for the whiskey turned out to be tumblers, and when our hosts arrived smartly attired, they lined up for their drinks. I have never seen such large measures of whiskey being dispensed before, and the evening continued in the same manner that it started. All the whiskey was consumed, and at the end of the evening, our hosts thanked us for everything and walked out ramrod straight without stumbling! Later Maren educated me as to Norwegian drinking habits and the cost of such excellent whiskey in Norway—little wonder that they felt obliged to make the most of such an opportunity.

———— ◦ ————

January 1980 brought an exciting event as my navigator, Ken Wood, and I flew over to a weapons firing range off the Welsh coast. I had already fired a Sidewinder, but this time I got to fire a Skyflash which was the British updated version of the American Sparrow all aspect, radar guided missile. It was quite an experience feeling the missile come off the Phantom and then seeing it in front of the nose as it proceeded to make a strong correction in the vertical before levelling off to intercept the target head on—success again!

May 1980 saw me clocking up the magic 2,000 hours on the F4 Phantom. What a remarkably versatile aircraft it was, with tremendous ruggedness and great wartime survivability as proved during the Vietnam war; I felt great pride to have flown such a capable aircraft for so long.

In July 1980, Pete Gray and I were on our way to Jever, a German Air Force base in the far north of Germany to participate in a three week course called the Tactical Leadership Programme. That course was just magic! The plan was for the NATO nations to send eighteen aircraft, twelve air-to-ground aircraft, and six air defence aircraft on each course. The course started with a period of ground school and then we were into the flying phase.

After some initial medium level air combat flying, we moved into the low level overland environment and stayed there for the remainder of the course. The role of the air defence aircraft was to detect and attack the large formations of air-to-ground aircraft as they simulated being on their inbound run to their target. The flying gave valuable exposure to the air defence crews of attacking a variety of different types of ground attack aircraft, such as F111s, A10s, Mirages, F104s, Buccaneers, Jaguars and Harriers. On the other hand, the ground attack crews gained experience of defending against such capable aircraft as the F15, F16, and of course the Phantom. The mission profiles steadily increased in complexity, and towards the end, the American Aggressors were brought in on the act. The flying was truly amazing, and I felt my confidence growing with each mission.

On the gliding front, May 1978 saw me at Lasham to compete in the ASW17 in the Open Class Nationals, finishing 3rd after eight competition days. Ten days after the last competition day at Lasham, I was at Bicester on a very special assignment. Arrangements had been made for Prince Charles to have his first experience of gliding and I was to be his instructor. The two-seat Grob Twin Astir was given a comprehensive going over days before the scheduled day of the flight, and it was then quarantined in a corner of the hangar, being roped off to keep everybody away.

The plan for the day was to fly a 100 kilometre triangular course, and I flew over the route in a training motor glider to identify safe outlanding fields. I have often wondered how things would have gone if I had landed out with Prince Charles in a field. One can just imagine members of the public coming up to investigate and one of them saying "Has anybody ever told you that you are the spitting image of Prince Charles?"! On the day itself, the Prince arrived driving his Aston Martin DB5 with his private detective stretched out across the rear seat looking extremely relaxed. This was a private visit and there was only the official RAF photographer present to record the event so Prince Charles could relax and enjoy the day.

Predictably the British weather failed to cooperate and there was no way that we were going cross country. I tried to make the best out of the day that I could as we flew a number of aerotows and I introduced the Prince to glider aerobatics. It was immediately obvious that Prince Charles was a natural pilot and he just needed gentle guidance as to the differences involved in flying a glider. I did have one slightly anxious moment when the pull up for a loop wasn't quite hard enough and we were rapidly running out of energy before getting to the top of the manoeuvre. The concern was that if a glider falls down tail first it can put stresses on the controls that they are not designed to take.

Fortunately the nose came down and we built up speed in the normal way! After a number of flights I was wondering what else I could do as there had not been any thermals so far. I took a bit of a risk as it had not been approved, but I decided to simulate a competition finish from a task by accelerating from the top end of the airfield to carry out a high speed pass at very low level—I'm only flying with the future king of England! All went well.

On one of the final flights, as we flew downwind in readiness for our approach, we hit what seemed to be a thermal. I was in a bit of a quandary as we were below the normal minimum height for circling, but on the other hand this was likely to be the only thermal we were going to get that day. I decided to go for it; we connected with the thermal and climbed to nearly 3,000 feet. I was glad that I had decided to try it as it gave the Prince a brief look at what gliding is really about and that is soaring, given that I was never going to be able to expose him to cross country gliding.

I thoroughly enjoyed the day and I found Prince Charles to be immensely likeable and easy to relate to. He also had a good sense of humour, one example being when we went over to the hangar for our lunch break. The briefing room had been transformed into a room that was fit for a prince to partake of lunch and, as he entered the room ahead of me, he glanced around noting the linen table cloth and silver cutlery and, turning to me, said, "I suppose it's always like this?"!

———◇———

Two and a half weeks later my crew Albert Johnson, Al Farmer, and I were in central France to prepare for the World Gliding Championships at Chateauroux. As usual we struggled to get some decent sponsorship, but Steve White, one of the team pilots, flew for British Airways and he persuaded them to come to the party. I was to defend my title in the RAFGSA ASW17, and we had decided to go to the airfield where the French equivalent of the RAFGSA Centre was based for some early practice. The airfield was called Romorantin, and there was also a small civilian gliding club there, the location being some 50 kilometres from Chateauroux.

At that time the French government's financial support for service gliding was extensive, and it was jaw dropping when I first entered their hangar—high performance gliders everywhere, including some suspended from the hangar roof. We had planned to spend two weeks there before going for the official practice week at Chateauroux. Unfortunately the weather was distinctly uncooperative, and we saw an awful lot of rain. The three of us fettled away on the glider, helping our mental state at least. As in most sports at the highest level, psychology plays a vital role as I had discovered in Finland. I had thought about this aspect long before arriving in France, and I finally thought that nobody expected me to win again; that was sufficient to relieve the mental pressure.

Finally the weather cleared sufficiently for me to get some local soaring done, but that wasn't what I really needed. The last day gave the conditions that we had looked forward to and lots of gliders were positioned at the launch point. I just couldn't believe my eyes as each glider was secured and the pilot got into his car and headed off. Finally the penny dropped, they were going for the sacrosanct French lunch! My main concern then was that the tow pilot was about to do the same. I rushed over to him and pleaded for him to do just one tow before lunch. The French lunch is a very important occasion and can easily last for two hours, some red wine being consumed and even a cognac if it is somebody's birthday, which gets interesting when it is followed by committing aviation!

Fortunately the tow pilot agreed to do the one tow for me and it was with considerable relief that I got strapped in and proceeded to fly just under 740 kilometre. And so to Chateauroux for the official practice week. As in Finland, I managed to find a quiet, remote spot to pitch my tent for the championships, and I went to book in. On arrival at the registration desk, I was advised that I would have to change the competition number on the glider as the number "26" had already been taken. I couldn't believe it, but my crew and I had no choice but to set to with masking tape and paint to modify "26" to make it read "02". It was just as well that I was not superstitious. The conditions during the practice week were not great, but I did get one reasonable day when I flew a 540 kilometre task.

The organisation had put in place a good arrangement for catering. Although there was the official catering setup on the airfield, it was possible to take the meal tickets to local restaurants and get cash credit towards the final bill. My crew, Maren, and I had an amusing incident one evening at a local restaurant when the lady who was taking our orders kept looking at me; after a while, she came back to our table carrying the colour supplement of the UK's *Sunday Telegraph*. There had been a special report on the British Gliding Team in that issue, and she realised that I was the person in the photo. Needless to say we were looked after very well that evening! It was lovely to have Maren with me throughout the championships even if she wasn't crewing for me. She had left our two young children in the capable hands of my mother and sister up in Scotland.

———◦———

My championships didn't start auspiciously as I finished the first day in 17th place out of 24 Open Class pilots. The second day was better for me; I finished sixth which brought me up to 8th overall. The third day proved to be a very interesting day! As usual, the French task setters set the maximum length task for the forecast conditions. It was slow going but finally I was nearing home, albeit solidly below final glide height.

I then noticed a fire and a number of gliders circling low down in the smoke. I joined in the smoke near the top and was relieved to find some weak lift which I used until it just stopped. There were now no further options as all lift had definitely finished, so I set out for Chateauroux which I wasn't able to see at this stage.

I pinpointed my position and realised that this was going to be incredibly tight. In these days of GPS supplied instrumentation, the competition pilot is given extremely accurate information that makes the final glide a precision exercise. When I was flying this final glide, I used a map to confirm my position and then referred to what was basically a circular slide rule and applied an appropriate wind factor to come up with the height required. Any additional safety factor could then be added on, and the device, fondly called the "John Willy" as it was produced by top competition pilot John Williamson, was calibrated for gliders of various performance levels.

On this glide I could only see one other glider on my left and a bit lower than me which was an Open Class glider being flown by Bert Zegels of Belgium. I determined to fly the 17 as accurately as I could, caressing the controls smoothly following the remaining gentle movements of the air. Finally I could see the airfield perimeter fence in the distance, and it all looked totally impossible! I decided to continue flying smoothly and accurately, being aware of the fields immediately before the airfield in case I needed one of them at fairly short notice!

After some time, I could see that I was going to clear the boundary fence and after that was a large concrete taxiway, the only problem being that the finish line was still some two kilometres beyond the fence. I cleared the boundary and continued flying towards the finish line in the distance until my nerves could stand it no longer and I lowered the undercarriage to touch down and roll with sufficient energy to cross the finish line. I even had to apply some wheel brake to stop after the line just to show that I had some extra in hand!

Only a few observers saw my finish as it was obvious that there was little chance of anybody getting home. It was quite something to see number 02 on the finish board as the only finisher out of all three classes. I was slow on the fourth day which put me in 15th place for the day and third overall. This gives some idea as to how tight the points spread can be. The weather picked up on Day 5, and I finished the 570 kilometre task in third position for the day which put me back in the lead. Amazingly, the next day also saw me achieve third place over a 505 kilometre triangle and further consolidate my overall lead. The next five days saw me in daily placings of 8th, 5th, 5th, 2nd, and 3rd, each day being sufficient to hold my overall lead.

My Open Class teammate Bernie Fitchett was out of contention for the podium positions, so our Team Manager, Dickie Feakes, tasked him with assisting me to hold my lead on the final day and take the title. Bernie and I had developed a simple code and he started ahead of me, staying ahead of me for much of the task and reporting back position and conditions as inputs to my decision-making process. Such tactics are fully legal as long as the gliders are of the same class, assistance from a pilot flying in a different class not being allowed.

When I had won the championships in Finland there had only been two classes, the Open Class and the Standard Class. At Chateauroux there were three classes with the introduction of the 15 metre class, the only restriction for the designer being that the wingspan was not to exceed 15 metres; in effect, a mini Open Class. As I write, many more classes have been since been developed. The German pilot, Helmut Reichmann, took his second world title winning the 15 metre class in a one off glider called the SB11 that had been designed and produced by the German Braunschweig Akaflieg group of university engineering students.

The SB11 was an ambitious project, the main revolutionary aspect being the variable wing geometry which increased the wing area for slow speed circling flight and which could be retracted for high speed cruising. It was constructed entirely out of carbon fibre and was just too expensive to be put into production. The design accomplished everything that it set out to and Helmut reported that the forces involved with adjusting the extensive flaps were no more than with conventional flaps.

For myself, everything worked well and I retained my Open Class crown with a greater margin than in Finland, having been in the overall lead for the final seven competition days. My prize this time was a lovely French leather jacket! It had been a long, hard event, and I flew eleven competition days, made extra challenging by the policy of getting the maximum out of every day. There can be a tendency for start line tactics to play a part at many competitions with each pilot trying to gain an advantage over the other pilots. This practice was rendered redundant at Chateauroux as pilots just had to get going once the start line opened if they were to stand a chance of getting home.

The last day was marked in the British camp by the attendance of the British Air Attache who came over from Paris for the day, and Maren assisted with providing the hospitality. Once more we had a party going before we returned to England the next day with the trailer suitably adorned with messages that proudly announced what had been achieved, bringing about some responses from drivers in the United Kingdom in the form of hooting their horns in applause.

The British celebrations were tempered by the fact that we had lost a friend and fellow pilot during the event. One day in good weather conditions a supporting member of the British Team gained permission to conduct an aerobatics display offset from the main runway on which all the gliders were in position in readiness for takeoff. The weather conditions were good, but the pilot had not flown the type of aircraft before and during the sequence he lost control and crashed at the side of the grid of gliders, being killed instantly. Although he had not been a close friend of mine, it had a great impact on all of us, especially as the team pilots had to then get airborne and compete at the highest level.

Overall though the competition at Chateauroux had been excellent. The airfield had been used by the United States Air Force during World War II and was massive. It was great to be able to use one of the enormous hangars to safely store the gliders overnight. One unforeseen element was when we discovered that the runway surface was quite abrasive and a single take off wore a significant amount of metal from the ASW17's tailskid. We had brought a couple of spares, but it was obvious that they were not going to be enough for the entire championships. My crew put on their thinking caps and finally decided to use some pieces of file metal welded on to the tailskid—problem solved.

The 92.5% Banner.

The 1977 route for
the trans-American
Smirnoff Derby.

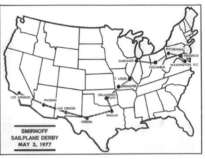

A proud day at Buckingham
Palace—receiving the MBE,
accompanied by Maren
and my mother.

Practising for the
World Gliding
Championships
in France.

Preparing to take HRH Prince Charles for his first flights in a glider.

.

Chapter 7

ACCOLADES AND ACCENTS

Those who honour me I will honour.
—1 Samuel 2:30, Holy Bible, NIV

———◄○►———

Less than a week after arriving back in the United Kingdom from France I was having my Phantom currency check, and ten days after that I was back instructing at Portmoak. The congratulatory letters and military signals that I received in the days and weeks after my arrival home were quite overwhelming. They were all special to me; but three that were particularly special were the two telegrams that came: one from Prince Philip in his capacity of Patron of the British Gliding Association and one from Prince Charles. The third one was a handwritten letter from Philip Wills, a man who had done so much for British gliding and who was not at all well at the time. I was also invited to attend a Sports Aid Foundation Celebrity Dinner in Newcastle, as well as the BBC's Sports Review of 1978 TV programme with Prince Charles in attendance.

A very special event took place in June 1979 when I was invited to attend a small private luncheon with The Queen and Prince Philip. There were only eight other guests including Claire Francis of yachting fame—it was all a great honour. Needless to say the guests arrived early and we were conducted to a large lounge room to await the arrival of Her Majesty. After a while we got an early warning when we heard the sound of barking corgis, and shortly afterwards The Queen entered the room.

The English are very good at organising such events and the staff ensured that only a small number of people were in the circle with The Queen at any time. When a guest had been there long enough, there was a discreet tap on the elbow to indicate that it was time to move out of the circle and let someone else in. The meal was, of course, excellent and most enjoyable once I got my nerves under control! The atmosphere was remarkably relaxed and The Queen and Prince Philip were gracious hosts.

There was time for further conversation in the same lounge room after lunch, and it was during this time that I had some precious utterly unforgettable moments with The Queen. Somehow the two of us ended up together by the huge bay window that looked up the Mall where preparations were taking place for a State visit the following week. We engaged in quite informal conversation for a while; it was almost as if we were neighbours having a chat! I didn't get to have time with Prince Philip but I have to say that The Queen was absolutely charming and came across as a very warm-hearted person. When I finally left the Palace, I was given my personal copy of the menu and seating plan. I was only sorry that Maren was not allowed to accompany me for such a special event.

———◦———

August 1979 saw me winning the Euroglide competition at Husbands Bosworth in Leicestershire in the trusty ASW17, and the year finished with a flourish when I was honoured to receive the Royal Aero Club's premier award, the Britannia Trophy. The trophy was awarded for the most commendable achievement in winged flight, and although it could be awarded annually, in practice that didn't always happen as the Royal Aero Club preferred to maintain the trophy's reputation for excellence. The award of the trophy to me was only the second time it had been awarded during the previous ten years. Previous recipients had included John Alcock, Sir Alan Cobham, Peter Twiss and Sheila Scott.

The year 1979 wrapped up with my attending a Man of the Year luncheon at the Savoy Hotel in London, being in the company of such figures as Sebastian Coe, J.P.R. Williams, and Stephen Hawking.

In 1980, Maren and I decided it was time to get into the housing market. We had been paying rent for too long and were seeing smart young university graduates joining the RAF and quickly getting into the buying and selling of houses. My squadron boss, Ian McBride, recommended the area near Cambridge due to the rental demand from American service personnel, so we bought a semi-detached house in St Ives about 11 miles from Cambridge.

—◇—

In September 1980, I had to attend a German course in preparation for my posting to Jever to be on the staff of the Tactical Leadership Programme. Maren was to have accompanied me, but there were no arrangements for Sonja and Brian to be looked after, so they all stayed in Scotland. They did, of course, join me in Jever, and we moved into the rental property that my predecessor had lived in. The house was in a small village called Hohenkirchen, about a fifteen minute drive from Jever town. As it turned out, we were the only foreigners in the village!

Maren quickly got to grips with the language as Norwegian had many similarities with German, so she enjoyed a reasonable social life. Sonja picked up German very quickly; she became fluent in next to no time, making many friends in the village, although she was more used to English with an American accent as she attended an American run international school. Brian attended a German kindergarten, and he had a teacher who could speak English. Maren cautioned her not to speak English or Brian would never get into speaking German. Brian observed proceedings for close to six months until he finally launched forth with his new language.

Although I had completed the German language course, I didn't actually need to use it in my job as both the staff members and the course participants were from a variety of European nations and the common language was, of course, English. Having written that, having some

German did come in quite useful socially, even if many of the words that I knew were military words! The local dialect took a bit of getting used to as the German that the locals spoke was heavily influenced by Dutch, East Friesland being close to the Dutch border.

The climate of the region was challenging as the terrain was completely flat and we seemed to experience more than our fair share of wind. We gained the impression that winter lasted six months! That written, we were not far from the local beaches and they were beautiful. Germans from the industrialised parts of Germany came up to the East Friesland beaches to enjoy the relatively pure air that blew in from the North Sea. People just had to accept that wind was a regular feature of life in northern Germany and they adapted life on the beach to accommodate it. It was quite amusing at first to see what looked like modified laundry baskets on the beach that people sat on. In fact, they were effective in combating the wind as the high backs gave the occupant good shelter.

It took awhile for the locals to accept us, but when they did, they showed us great hospitality and friendship. We had brought our old Audi over from the United Kingdom, and it continued to give us good service, although driving a right hand drive vehicle on the wrong side of the road took some getting used to. Towards the end of the tour of duty, Maren and I drove down to southern Germany to the Mercedes factory to collect a brand-new car. One of the perks of doing an overseas tour was that British service personnel could purchase a new vehicle free of duty as long as it was owned in the United Kingdom afterwards for a specified minimum period of time. Another perk of the job was that Maren and I had access to an American facility that had a great range of stuff, particularly Texas-sized steaks! They made the road and ferry journey to get to the facility worth it.

———◦———

Part of the job specification was that I was to remain current on the Phantom even though the tour of duty at Jever was classed as a ground tour, so I drove down to RAF Wildenrath to get some flying in between Tactical Leadership Programme (TLP) courses. The squadrons were pretty hard pressed to meet their own tasking, and I was very grateful to get the flying that they so willingly gave me. The end of the year provided me with an unexpected award from my years on 43 Squadron in the form of a Queen's Commendation for Valuable Service in the Air.

The work at TLP was pretty well full on during the courses, but there were compensations as the various nations were encouraged to send along two seat versions of their aircraft so that TLP staff members could get airborne on the missions and thereby deliver more effective debriefs afterwards. I got to fly in the F104, Mirage 5, F16, Alpha Jet, and F15. My favourite was undoubtedly the F15, and I really wondered why the Royal Air Force hadn't purchased the type. The F16 had superb performance, but the F15 also had excellent performance coupled with a wonderful air-to-air radar system. It also had beautiful handling; you may be gaining the impression that I really liked the aircraft! At one point during my tour with TLP, I was able to get airborne in an AWACS aircraft which was extremely impressive in its surveillance role.

One of the major drawbacks to being posted to Jever was that my gliding was going to take a major hit. I did very little gliding apart from competitions, but my sights were really set on defending my Open Class title in 1981, the selected location for the championships being Paderborn-Haxterberg in northern Germany. The decision to hold the championships at Paderborn was not without controversy as it was not in the area of Germany that offered the best soaring conditions.

I did get a feel for the site and area during the Pre-Worlds in August 1980, but my thoughts were very much on what glider I was going to be flying the following year. I knew that Gerhard Waibel was working on a successor to the ASW17 and that it was going to be designated the ASW22 (the letters AS standing for Alexander Schleicher and the "W" standing for Waibel). I also knew that they would let me fly the first aircraft in the World Championships, but the timing was always going to be very tight. Open Class gliders were just about to undergo a radical change in performance levels, and I also knew that Klaus Holighaus, the owner of the Schempp-Hirth factory in southern Germany, was working on a replacement for the Nimbus2. The workers at Schleichers were working overtime to try and get the first 22 in the air in time for the big event, and early in 1981, Maren, the children, and I went down to the Schleicher factory with our caravan to urge everybody on!

One of the good memories I have of that time was first thing in the morning when Gerhard Waibel arrived at the front of our caravan in his vintage Porsche to deliver some fresh croissants from the local bakery. Things didn't go according to plan as, probably because of the extra pressure, a worker made a mistake which put everything back. The manager of the factory, Edgar Kremer, called a business breakfast and broke the bad news to me. Although half expecting the news, it was a shock as I knew that the older generation Open Class gliders would be outclassed by the new gliders. I thought rapidly and asked if I could use the phone. I rang Klaus Holighaus and he told me that he had been expecting my call! He very graciously said that he would see what he could do for me. He was as good as his word, and I ended up flying at Paderborn with one of the first three sets of Nimbus3 wings.

In April 1981 I went down to the Hahnweide airfield, the local airfield to the Schempp-Hirth factory, and Klaus kindly let me fly his Nimbus3 for a couple of flights that yielded some ten hours, albeit limited cross country flying due to the weather conditions. A couple of days later I was at the Iserlohn Rheinmark airfield to fly Bruno Gantenbrink's Nimbus3, and I had a good flight of 660 kilometres. It was obvious that the new breed of Open Class gliders would have a significant performance advantage over the older gliders.

The official practice week at Paderborn didn't give great soaring conditions apart from one day when I set off on a 1,000 kilometre task. The conditions were not as good as forecast and I turned back from the first turnpoint for a distance of 780 kilometres. By now I was feeling comfortable with the Nimbus3's handling even though it was so different from the old ASW17. My accommodation for Paderborn was different from the other two championships as I was able to arrange to use a room on a nearby military base.

Again I had thought about the psychological aspects of the championships, and I simply reasoned that nobody but nobody expected me to win three in a row as it had never been done before.

The first day of the World Championships saw me landing out in weak conditions but my distance was enough to put me in second place. The conditions were better the next day, and I won the day which put me in the overall lead. The next day was very poor and I landed back at Paderborn; it ended up being a no contest day. The weather conditions on Day 3 were also poor, but I had an even greater problem! As I was local soaring pre-start, I discovered that I had a significant instrument problem that was bad enough for me not to be happy to go out on task. With a heavy heart I made a radio call to my crew, Albert and Stu Mulholland, to advise them that I was returning.

Paderborn had a single east/west grass strip and it was not a large airfield; there was no avoiding the fact that my arrival was going to be very public! The championships organisation had done a great job in putting in a large grandstand type structure to maximise the viewing experience of the public. Gliding was and is a popular sport in Germany with a large number of participants, and there were a good number of people who came each day to watch the action. There was also a considerable media presence; and as I came to a halt in front of the grandstand, the TV camera crews came out to film everything! I got out of the cockpit and just let my crew get on with the task of resolving the problem as I tried to appear relaxed. Actually I was very conscious of the time ticking away and the fact that Klaus and Bruno, who were pairs flying, had already started the task.

Finally my crew secured the instrument panel and declared their confidence that all was now well. I got airborne again and headed out on task hoping to make the best of the day and putting the memory of what had just happened behind me. In fact, the day turned out better than I had expected and I came in second for the day which secured my overall lead. I won the next two days and remained in the overall lead. The next day brought heavy showers and it ended up being a zero point day. I landed out on the following day, ending up in 7ᵗʰ position for the day but still in the overall lead.

The next day was pretty dramatic! The conditions were dreadful and I just couldn't see how we were going to be launched into what looked like a dead sky. The organisation decided to cancel one class but the other two were duly launched. Somehow I managed to struggle around the first turnpoint of the small triangle and ended up landing near the second turnpoint. I thought I was ahead of everybody but when I made the telephone call to Crew Control, I was told to prepare myself for some bad news. I don't know how, but somehow Klaus Holighaus had managed to get halfway up the final leg and that performance resulted in his taking over the overall lead with just one day to go.

The conditions for the final day were also very weak, and I struggled to get sufficient altitude to make a start. Klaus had been shadowing me but suddenly he wasn't there and eventually I got high enough to get going. I wasn't seeing any other gliders but when I was about halfway down the final leg of the triangle I suddenly got the feeling that I wasn't alone! Looking behind me I saw Klaus a bit lower than I was. It was now a question of gliding out for distance. Klaus saw a small ridge to one side and he diverted to it hoping to get some weak lift but it wasn't working and he landed in the area.

I got a small amount of assistance from a factory chimney and then glided out for my own outlanding. I knew that I had gone farther than Klaus—but was it enough to take back the lead and clinch the victory? In fact, the extra distance that I had secured over Klaus was enough to get me back into first position overall and confirmed the successful defence of my Open Class title, becoming the first person in history to win three consecutive world championships. It took awhile for it all to really sink in but I had made history; and whatever happened in the future, that would not be taken from me.

Psychologically the World Championships at Paderborn were much harder than the championships in France. On the face of it, one could be forgiven for thinking it would be easier as there were less fully competitive gliders in the Open Class. Klaus Holighaus, Bruno Gantenbrink and I were flying the three Nimbus3s, but Dick Butler from the States had extensively modified his ASW17 in collaboration with Gerhard Waibel. He constructed inner wing stubs which extended the wingspan to 23 metres and made the glider fully competitive.

I guess the championships were challenging for me psychologically because of the mainly weak conditions and the fact that I was up against two extremely capable German pilots who were pairs flying and working closely together. The final day was nerve wracking but the outcome was good for me.

After the prize-giving, the three class winners were given a flight in a hot air balloon. I had never flown in a hot air balloon, and I thoroughly enjoyed the experience, apart from the landing which was somewhat less than graceful as there was quite a stiff breeze blowing. Maren had been able to come down to Paderborn for the final few days of the championships as my mother had come over to look after the children. On our arrival back to Hohenkirchen we were caught by surprise as the village had laid on an amazing party to welcome us back, including the local musicians playing in our lounge room!

Later in 1981 I travelled to South Africa to fly in their Nationals. The conditions were of course much stronger than in Europe and I enjoyed the challenge finishing second overall, the experience being marred by the glider that I was flying sustaining damage in an outlanding due to pilot error.

In April 1982 my family and I went to Marpingen in Germany to join the German training camp for their top pilots. It was during the Easter holidays and we stayed in our caravan and froze as there were snow showers to cope with. My German wasn't up to the ground lectures, but it was good to have been part of it and to fly with three-time World Champion Helmut Reichmann—six World titles in the same glider!

The year 1982 was an extremely important year because I made a decision jointly with Maren that would determine the rest of our lives. I was on a permanent commission with the Royal Air Force which meant that I had a guaranteed career until the age of 55; however, I had an option point at the age of 38 whereby I could leave the service. Military living can be challenging for all sorts of reasons and it can be hard for children as they typically change schools and have to make new friends every two to three years. Many military parents decide to send their children to boarding school to give them continuity of education and friendships, but Maren and I didn't want to do this, not to mention the fact that Sonja and Brian didn't want to go to boarding school!

So in November 1982, I signed a paper declaring my intention to leave the Royal Air Force (RAF) one year later at the age of 38. This was a huge decision as I was giving up pretty well 100 percent security—and I was earning a reasonable salary by United Kingdom standards. Moreover, in 1982-1983, the UK was solidly in a major recession and none of the airlines were hiring pilots. Senior RAF officers would ask me the question: "Have you thought this through?" Whilst showing a confident public face, I did have moments of grave doubt as to whether I had really made a sensible decision. Anyway I stuck to the decision and I was advised that I could change my mind during the year before I was due to leave without a problem. I was further advised that if I changed my mind during the first year after I left the RAF, I would be able to rejoin. This gave me a degree of security with what I was embarking on, and I was thankful that there was a shortage of fast jet pilots!

The year 1982 finished with a flourish when I was awarded the Lilienthal Medal by Prince Andrew, the President of the Royal Aero Club. The Lilienthal Medal is gliding's highest award and its award meant and still means a great deal to me. I received the medal, not only for the first ever hat trick at World Championships, but also for other services to gliding.

In 1983 I left Germany to fly in the Open Class Nationals at Lasham in the United Kingdom and flew the RAFGSA's Nimbus3 to first place.

My sights were now set on the next World Championships which were scheduled to be held in Argentina in 1983. That was until the Falklands conflict fired up in 1982 and plans had to be changed. The Americans put their hand up and offered to host the championships at Hobbs, New Mexico, and so it was agreed.

I was left alone as far as operational service in the Falklands was concerned as I was on a ground tour in spite of remaining current on type; in fact, the Phantoms were never involved in the shooting war as the Harriers were.

My plan leading up to the big event at Hobbs was to get practice in at the Odessa airfield in Texas, the conditions being representative of what I could expect at Hobbs. The RAF obligingly assisted getting the British team gliders over to Odessa in a Hercules aircraft as part of a training mission. I had eight flights at Odessa, but the main emphasis was on getting the big Nimbus and its systems in good order in readiness for Hobbs. I felt ready for the big event, and we moved over to the enormous World War II airfield. Four practice flights later, and I was into the championships.

The weather over the duration of the championships was exceptionally good, apart from some thunderstorm activity, and this was reflected in the high task speeds. My first two days saw me finish in 6th and 8th position, but then came the disaster day. Thunderstorms had been forecast for the day, but they built up earlier in the task area than had been expected. My Open Class team mate Bernie Fitchett and I started too late, and we got caught by a huge storm in the vicinity of the second turnpoint, resulting in us both landing out.

The majority of the Open Class competitors made it round the task which made it even more disastrous in terms of our points for the day, my scoring only 185 points in comparison to the winner's 1,000 points. I was furious with myself, and the next day my hair was on fire. The Open Class was set a 522 kilometre triangle, and I went around the course at an achieved speed of 178.1 kph, the fastest speed ever flown at a World Championships. Although I won the day, it didn't do that much for me in the overall standings, and I knew that I had blown the championships. My overall performance was not of a high standard, and I ended up in tenth position.

The 18th World Gliding Championships at Hobbs was tremendously successful, and the organisation could take pride in running an outstanding event over twelve competition days, especially given the short notice to get it all together.

I did have some consolation in 1983 when I received the Air League Founders' Medal from Prince Philip their patron. The medal is for meritorious achievement in the whole field of British aviation and, as with the Britannia Trophy, has not been awarded every year. Again I was in the company of people such as astronauts Armstrong, Aldrin, and Collins, the Red Arrows, and Freddie Laker.

NNNN
ZCZC BAX419 LFK115 JWC
ZXRH CO GRLF 038
BUCKINGHAMPALACE/LONDON/LF 38/35 9 1300

SQUADRON LEADER D G LEE MBE RAF
NATO FIGHTER LEADER SCHOOL GERMAN AIR FORCE
JEVER
BFP027

WARMEST CONGRATULATIONS TO MY GLIDING INSTRUCTOR ON HIS
SPECTACULAR AND UNIQUE ACHIEVEMENT FROM AN ADMIRING, IF
INCONSTANT PUPIL
            CHARLES

COL BFP027

NNNN

Telegram
from Prince Charles after
the historic three in a row win.

336081 PO BM G
299992 PO TS G
N139 BUCKINGHAM PALACE 33/30 09 1815

MICHAEL CARLTON ESQ
C/O THE BRITISH GLIDING ASSOCIATION KIMBERLEY HOUSE BOURNE WAY
LEICESTER

FROM THE DUKE OF EDINBURGH.
PLEASE GIVE GEORGE LEE MY WARMEST CONGRATULATIONS ON A
MAGNIFICENT ACHIEVEMENT
            PHILIP

COL NIL

Telegram from Prince Philip
as Patron of the BGA
following the victory.

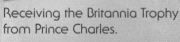

Receiving the Britannia Trophy
from Prince Charles.

Receiving the Lilienthal
Medal from Prince Andrew.

Receiving the
Air League's Founders' Medal
from Prince Philip.

Chapter 8

DEPARTURES AND ARRIVALS

Life belongs to the living, and he who lives
must be prepared for changes.
—Johan Wolfgang von Goethe

———◦———

Just as my gliding seemed to be winding down, at least at the World Championships level, Maren and I were faced with a major challenge as we agreed that I would indeed leave the Royal Air Force on my 38th birthday. As I have already written, a serious recession was still in full force and no United Kingdom airline was hiring pilots. I wrote a large number of letters to the domestic airlines, but most didn't even respond and those that did indicated that I was too old!

Enter Tug Willson again. Tug and I had kept in contact since he left the RAF at his 38th birthday, and he had written on one occasion that he would help me get into Cathay Pacific Airways one day. I had laughed at the time as I had no intention then of leaving the service. Now things were different, and I contacted Tug to find out if there was any chance of being employed by Cathay Pacific. It turned out that there was a slim chance, and he recommended that Maren and I travel to Hong Kong to have a look around. That was a very good suggestion as I had been to Hong Kong before in the Phantom, but Maren had never been.

We tried to get out on a standby basis with the RAF, but we were getting nowhere; I ended up purchasing two tickets at short notice with Air Lanka. On our arrival into Hong Kong, two things hit us. One was the unbelievable humidity as we had arrived in August, the worst month of the whole year as both temperature and humidity reach their peaks. The second thing was the noise level wherever we went as Cantonese is not the quietest of languages. Tug's wife, Marlene, collected us from the airport and we drove out to their home in a quiet part of the New Territories.

As we were enjoying a cup of tea, the phone rang and Marlene announced that it was for me! This came as a bit of a shock as I didn't think anybody knew about my arrival apart from Tug and Marlene. Tug was away on a flight but, unbeknown to me, before he left he had arranged for me to have a simulator assessment—the phone call was to confirm the arrangements. I couldn't believe it, but Tug filled me in on all the details on his return. I later found out that Tug had spoken up for me at management level as he knew me so well. To consider hiring me was a big step for the company as I would be the first ex-fighter pilot without any transport flying experience that they had hired. I would also have been considered old at 38!

Subsequent to my being hired, that all changed and many 38-year-old ex-fighter pilots were brought on board. This period brought about a fundamental change in the way the company looked at their hiring policy. Previously they had only considered aircrew who had thousands of hours of transport flying experience in their logbooks, but now there was a realisation that they needed to take a closer look at the man and not just the logbook.

Tug was a Training Captain on the TriStar fleet and, as the assessment was to take place in the TriStar simulator, he was able to give me a detailed briefing on what to expect. The simulator session went well; and when it was all over, I was told not to read too much into it, but as I was in Hong Kong I may as well do a technical quiz, have a medical examination, and be formally interviewed! All of this went well, and I was requested to keep the company updated with my progress on getting my Air Transport

Pilot's License (ATPL) as I had planned to start doing the ground school and flying at Oxford on my return to the United Kingdom. Having gone through all of that, Maren and I set about enjoying what remained of our brief visit to Hong Kong.

————◦►————

On our return to the United Kingdom, I set off to commence my studies and flying training at Oxford's Kidlington airport, my intention being to live in the Officers' Mess at nearby RAF Benson. After a while I found out that it was a particularly noisy Officers' Mess and I was falling behind the sleep/work drag curve. I decided that drastic action was needed if I was to do all that I needed to do and I rang a gliding friend, John Delafield, who lived in a small country village on the other side of Oxford to ask if it would be ok for me to stay with him and his wife Jane for the duration of my studies. I was so thankful for their positive response, and I moved over to their house without delay.

Now I was in business as their house was away from main roads and was beautifully quiet. I established a daily schedule in coming back from my studies, having a quick cup of tea and a chat with Jane, and then shutting myself into the dining room for some serious heads down time. It all worked beautifully and I got through the examinations and the necessary flying tests. As an ex-fighter pilot I was not given any exemptions; I had to do a lot of flying in the Seneca twin. Even in 1983 the hourly rate for the Seneca was very expensive but I had a wonderful female flying instructor who was conscious of what every minute was costing me and she used our time in the air most efficiently.

I had been updating Cathay Pacific on my progress, and when I got the Air Transport Pilot's License in my hand, I rang Hong Kong again. I had been dealing with a particular manager, and he advised me that they would be putting me on a B747 course in April 1984. I was now back with Maren and the children in our house in St Ives and two nights after that call to Hong Kong the phone rang at 1.00AM, that time equating to office opening in Hong Kong. It was a different manager this time, but I knew him from the interviewing process. He started the conversation by asking if I still wanted to join Cathay Pacific; I was now fully awake! I confirmed that I did, and he then asked me if I could be in Hong Kong in ten days time to start a conversion course on the B747. I asked him if he would hold, I had a hurried few words with Maren to confirm that she could cope with everything in the UK, and I responded in the affirmative. So in January 1984, I headed over to Hong Kong leaving Maren and the children in the UK for them to finish their school year.

On my arrival in Hong Kong, I was accommodated in the nearby airport hotel and quickly started into the ground school studies. It was an interesting time to come to Hong Kong as the future of the territory had not been decided, the then British Prime Minister Margaret Thatcher not yet having had her talks with the Chinese leadership. Confidence was at a very low ebb and the Hong Kong dollar was weakening rapidly. The extreme lack of confidence was reflected in the property market, and I saw an opportunity to get into the market at a favourable price. I'm sure that my actions raised the odd eyebrow on the management floor of Cathay Pacific as I had only just started my studies, but I had not come to Hong Kong to fail! So I purchased a detached house on a nice estate in the middle of the New Territories, it being the second house that I had bought without Maren having seen it first.

Hong Kong could be considered as being divided into three main areas: Hong Kong Island where the financial institutions and most expensive properties were located, Kowloon across the water on the southern tip of the mainland, and the New Territories which was the largest area leading up to the Chinese border. In view of the mortgage expense, I had to move out of the airport hotel and into the house which was new and had never been lived in. I was now faced with commuting to work, but the public transport system in Hong Kong was excellent, there being a shuttle bus from the estate where I lived to connect with an electric railway which in turn connected with an underground system. It all worked efficiently with regular services and everything being squeaky clean—no graffiti in Hong Kong. In fact Hong Kong boasts a public transport travelling rate in excess of 90 percent, the highest in the world. Although we did purchase a car later, primarily for travelling across the New Territories, there was little point in travelling downtown by car as the roads were extremely congested, journey times were unpredictable, and car parking rates in town were extortionate.

Living in quite a large house with only basic decoration and minimal furniture was an experience. Cooking was not, and is still not my forte, so I ate well when on flights away and existed on tinned food and rice when at home. I needed some domestic assistance to keep the house in order, and I can still recall the face of the Chinese cleaning lady as she went around the house wondering how anybody could be living there. I had a borrowed table and chair, a second hand fridge and a bed! I would ring Maren whilst lying in bed and looking at the moon through a large curtainless window, the sound of my voice echoing around the house.

The back garden came up against what was basically jungle and, as the house had never been lived in, there was some serious weeding to be done. Maren did travel to Hong Kong during my training for a short visit to see me and the house I had bought. We then decided on a colour scheme for the house and organised some more furniture. When Maren left to return to the United Kingdom, I engaged a team of Chinese workers to undertake the interior painting of the house. The workers were under a supervisor who thankfully spoke reasonable English.

One day I had returned home after a flight and the workers were just about to take their lunch break. The supervisor invited me to join them so we all went off to a Chinese restaurant in the nearby town for some dim sum. It didn't really matter that the workers couldn't speak English as the noise level in the restaurant precluded any sensible conversation. After a while the old Chinese lady came to our table with the dim sum trolley and various small food items magically appeared on my plate. I was doing ok until the chickens' feet appeared in front of me and I baulked at trying to extract some non-existent meat from the bone, grizzle and skin.

The ground school and simulator training finally finished, and it was time to get to grips with a 747. I will never forget that first circuit training session on the 747. My instructor was Frank Seaton, and he must have had nerves of steel as we conducted the training at Hong Kong's Kai Tak airport using runway 13, the approach to which involved the famous late final turn in front of the visual marker chequerboard. Runway 13 extended towards the open sea so it was the preferred option, weather and wind permitting. Landing an aircraft the size of the 747 was very different from landing a Phantom as I was so far above the mainwheels when they touched the runway, although the Flight Engineer aided the process by calling out the final tens of feet using the output from a radio altimeter whose sensor was located on the mainwheel assembly. Although I had been used to flying with a navigator on the Phantom, the crew concept and procedures on the 747 were very new for me and the whole experience that day was challenging and draining, but it was also exhilarating.

At the end, I walked down the steps, looked back at the huge aircraft, and felt 10 feet tall! The 747 is a magnificent aircraft with superb handling for its size. Everything was on a different scale to what I had been used to: the amount of power that the four Rolls Royce engines produced, the fact that I would be taking in excess of 400 passengers to some distant location, and that I could be taking off at a weight of just over 370 tons and landing at times at a weight of over 285 tons greatly impressed me.

While I was doing the line training, the flights were mostly local and of fairly short duration; but once I was checked out, I started being rostered for the long haul flights. The longest sectors at that time were Hong Kong to Vancouver and return, and Hong Kong to London and return. These ultra long haul westbound flights in winter could approach fourteen hours in duration due to the strong headwinds. Fuel was always tight on these routes, but it was the exception for a diversion to take place. Often our route to Europe would take us over the western end of the Himalayas which required a very high minimum safety altitude for terrain clearance. That was fine for normal operations, but we had to have a pre-planned escape route to be used in the event of a pressurisation failure. This route involved us flying away from the normal airway and descending over lower terrain to divert to an unfamiliar airfield in Russia. I think we all held our breath as we flew along that fortunately short part of the route!

Two other major challenges were a lack of take-offs and landings, and jetlag. As an ex-fighter pilot I really felt the lack of landings in a typical month; and in fact later on, the company changed their approach in how they accommodated ex-fighter pilots by putting them on the TriStar fleet which operated the local services and offered lots of take-offs and landings. The other challenge was jetlag and this was fairly alien for me. Going to bed and trying to get some sleep in the afternoon knowing that I would be flying through the night was one thing, but working out what might be best at the other end in terms of routine when confronted with an eight hour time difference was another. It was even worse when I flew to Vancouver as that involved crossing the International Date Line; in terms of keeping Hong Kong time on the watch, we would sometimes land before we took off! I always found coping with jetlag to be easier westbound than eastbound; but overall, jetlag is something that the human body is not designed for.

We always had a "heavy" crew for the long haul flights; that is we had an additional First Officer and an additional Flight Engineer so that everybody got some rest away from the flight deck. I flew the "Classic" 747 which was not really optimised for long haul flying, but we did have two basic bunk beds behind a curtain on the upper deck immediately behind the flight deck. I found it very difficult to get any sleep during my scheduled break unless I was extremely tired, the other aspect being that there were fare-paying passengers on the small upper deck as well. The later version of the 747, the 747-400, was optimised for long haul flying and crews had a small bedroom for their rest period. The longest flight that we did with a standard crew was Hong Kong to Auckland, the flight time for which could be in excess of nine and a half hours, with a departure time from Hong Kong around 11.00PM. The sun would be rising as we approached the northern coast of Australia and we would all start feeling better. The problem was that there was another four hours or so of flying still to go! We all learned to cope with these challenges, the main aim being to feel on top when the pressure was on during the final approach and landing.

———◄○►———

The security situation was so different during the 1980s and '90s, and it was good to be able to invite a passenger to the flight deck who had expressed interest in seeing what went on. Occasionally, as a Captain, I would invite a passenger to return to the flight deck to observe the approach and landing, but I was careful to be very selective. I believe such gestures enhanced public relations, and it gave some fare-paying members of the public a greater understanding of what went on at the "sharp end." Of course things are so different these days with bullet-proof, locked flight deck doors—a visit to the flight deck is truly a thing of the past. What was not appreciated by some visitors to the flight deck was that the timing of the visit had been carefully planned so that the workload was at a minimum. Such passengers would often go away thinking that aircrew had a life of Riley as they were free to chat and nothing much seemed to be going on. What they didn't see, of course, was the descent, possible holding, and final landing hours later when the weather conditions weren't good, fuel was tight, and maybe a technical problem or two all focussed the crew's minds.

Flying into Kai Tak was always challenging even under apparently benign conditions, but every pilot who knew it had a certain fondness for it. When weather conditions and other traffic permitted, air traffic would give a clearance to carry out a so-called visual step down approach. When inbound from the north or east, this meant flying a visual curved arrival around the south side of Hong Kong Island and across the harbour for a late turn onto finals, thus saving a considerable amount of time and fuel. It was also great fun!

———◄○►———

I joined Cathay Pacific at the beginning of a non-stop expansion for the airline. That expansion continued throughout my time with the company and it has continued ever since with an apparently ever increasing route network as more and more aircraft were purchased. When I joined Cathay, the airline was relatively small and everybody pretty well knew everybody else. By the time I left the company, it had grown to become a big player and inevitably it became harder to know people.

Layover times down route varied according to the scheduled pattern, but during the early years of expansion there were some very attractive flights. The best one had to be when the company started flying to Auckland as it was only one flight per week and the crew who flew the aircraft down were left there until the next service arrived! As there was only the once a week service, there was no standby commitment, so effectively it was a mini holiday.

Maren came down with me on one of these flights, and we had a great time exploring the north island. In general Maren didn't accompany me on many flights although she did come with me to Bombay which certainly opened her eyes! One other occasion comes to mind when I was flying to Paris on a cargo aircraft schedule and Maren flew over on the passenger service. My pattern gave a couple of free days in Paris so we celebrated Maren's 40th birthday in style.

Later on, layover times were progressively reduced. Pattern lengths also varied, one of the freighter patterns lasting for just under a fortnight (two weeks) as the crew flew around Europe and the Middle East. Cathay had traditionally hired crews from the United Kingdom and Australia, but as the expansion gathered pace, the recruiting net was cast wider and crews were hired from New Zealand, Canada, and the United States. When I joined the company, crews were required to live in Hong Kong, but as the numbers grew overseas, basings became available. This suited many aircrew for their own personal reasons, but there were financial implications to be considered. Because of the pace of the expansion, I was considered for, and subsequently promoted to the rank of Captain in just under four years from joining the company.

After a number of years doing line flying, I became a Training Captain. I found training pilots to be immensely rewarding work and to have the satisfaction of seeing them become new Captains. Later I became a

Check Captain and finally a Senior Check Captain. Checking a pilot was, of course, quite different from the training task and, if a Captain was being checked, I would spend the flight on the observer's seat immediately behind the Captain's seat. Becoming a Senior Check Captain involved conducting circuit training sessions as pilots were converted onto type. That was very challenging work as some pilots coped better than others! Although some of the circuit training was conducted at Hong Kong, it was preferred to use Canton (Guangzhou) as it was close by, there was less traffic, and the landing fees were less. Occasionally we would use the then Portuguese colony of Macau for our training. Check and training flying was mostly on the shorter regional routes and although it meant my going to work more frequently, my body thanked me for the change!

——◁◦▷——

I joined Cathay Pacific in January 1984, and Maren and the children joined me in August the same year. I had bought a small, second hand, slightly rusting Japanese hatchback car for transport so I was able to proudly collect them from the airport and show the children the house that I had bought. A priority was to organise education for the children, Sonja being 11 and Brian being just under 8. We were fortunate in having a very good international school for primary education as part of the estate where we lived, so we enrolled Brian there.

Hong Kong being a British territory at the time, there was an organisation called the English Schools Foundation (ESF) and there was an excellent ESF school within comfortable commuting distance for Sonja. The standard of the ESF school was very impressive, and we put this down to the calibre of the motivated teaching staff who wanted to work on the other side of the world. Sonja and Brian both went through their secondary education in Hong Kong with very good results, and Maren and I felt that the education system was a definite plus.

During his school years in Hong Kong, Brian went on two trips to Nepal that had been organised by the school. The first time he became quite ill over there, but he enjoyed everything else so much that he put his hand up to go a second time! Just after finishing his final secondary level examination, Brian went off to Ibiza, an island owned by Spain, for a celebratory holiday with his friends. While over there, he met a girl from Hungary, Diana, and on his return he announced to Maren and me that he had met the girl he would be marrying! We naturally thought it had been just a holiday romance, but when we commented to Brian to that effect, he burst into tears and said he meant it. We were to have cause to recall his words later! In due course, both of our children went on to attend university in the United Kingdom, Sonja to Southampton and Brian to Portsmouth.

A Cathay Pacific 747
landing at Kai Tak airport
Hong Kong.

Chapter 9

Hong Kong Living

Variety's the very spice of life;
that gives it all the flavour.
—William Cowper

———◄○►———

When I arrived in Hong Kong, I attended church on a nearby Royal Air Force base which operated helicopters. In due course this connection led me to become an honorary member of the Officers' Mess, and Maren and I enjoyed the associated social life. There was also a very good casual Indian eating establishment on the base which served up excellent food as long as we didn't think about the surroundings too much.

The average visitor to Hong Kong spent 2.3 days there, and never got beyond all that downtown had to offer, mostly shopping, markets and restaurants. In fact, Hong Kong has a lot of variety and things to see and do. Hong Kong is truly an amazing place, the sort of place that would have to be invented if it didn't exist. The official population was between 6 and 7 million, but everybody reckoned that it was actually much higher because of the number of illegal immigrants.

On arriving in Hong Kong, the first thing that struck me was the number of high rise buildings. The next thought that came to me was, "I hope the engineers have got their sums right!" I knew that Hong Kong was hit regularly by typhoons in late summer which of course was the same meteorological feature as the hurricane or cyclone, just a different name. In fact the high rise buildings, some up to 40 floors high, coped just fine with the at times frighteningly strong wind gusts, just swaying a bit but without any structural damage. The year before I arrived in Hong Kong, the territory had been hit by a particularly strong typhoon, Typhoon Ellen. Quite large boats had been picked up from the sea and tossed onto dry land, as well as there being a considerable amount of structural damage on less well constructed buildings. Typhoon conditions impacted the whole territory as schools were closed and the public transport system was shut down. Naturally that included the famous Star Ferry which operated between Kowloon and Hong Kong Island.

Flying operations in and out of Kai Tak airport could be challenging indeed if there was a typhoon in the vicinity, especially if there was a very strong tailwind down the instrument approach leading into the late visual turn onto runway 13. Of course if conditions were deemed to be too risky, the decision was made to divert inbound aircraft and even hold aircraft on the ground until conditions improved.

Hong Kong is at a sub-tropical latitude and does experience four distinct seasons in the year. Surprisingly it did get quite cold in winter, felt all the more as the houses were constructed with heat in mind more than cold. In general, late autumn and winter gave the dry conditions when high pressure systems would form over China and the flow across the territory brought down the drier air.

In the early years that would be the nicest time of the year with plenty of dry conditions and sunshine; unsurprisingly that was when the greatest number of tourists came. As the years went by, however, the ever increasing number of new factories in southern China made their presence felt by the atmospheric pollution that was swept across the territory. By the time I left Hong Kong in January 1999, the pollution in winter had become so bad that Hong Kong Island was just a misty outline across the harbour. Transitioning from winter into spring brought increasing humidity, but it always seemed to be cold around Chinese New Year as well.

Chinese New Year was the major holiday time for the locals, and millions went on the move to visit family members on the mainland. It was not unusual for businesses and shops to close for up to a fortnight at this time. Temperature and humidity steadily increased through the summer months reaching a peak in time for the typhoon season. Frayed tempers were much in evidence by the time August came around. Some people struggled with the high humidity and made a point of being in air conditioning as much as possible.

Maren and I thought that would make coping with it even harder, and we just accepted the fact that we would sweat during the day, but we did close up the house and appreciate our air conditioning during the evenings. Apparently houses built in the 1970s were generally not air conditioned and I wonder how people managed to get a decent night's sleep during the summer months. One of the most physically challenging flights was to fly down to Melbourne, Australia, in August when the Hong Kong humidity was at its worst and Melbourne was still in winter and be there for a couple of days before flying back. When I got off the aircraft in Hong Kong, it was like being enveloped by a hot, soggy blanket. After a few years in Hong Kong, we decided that we would get a swimming pool installed in our back garden; that certainly brought about an improved quality of life.

The year after I arrived in Hong Kong, my stepfather died. The following year, 1986, my mother wrote me a letter in which she shared that she wanted a completely new start. She had always liked our small house in the United Kingdom, and she wondered if it would be possible for her to leave Ireland to live in it. Maren and I agreed to her request, and I gave the tenants the required notice. My sister June and her husband moved up from the south of England to live in the same town, and I was happy that my mother would receive the important daily support.

———◇———

Hong Kong was surprisingly hilly, and we enjoyed some good hill walking on the hill that was directly behind our estate. A range of hills separated Kowloon from the New Territories, the most well-known feature of it being the so-called Lion Rock because the outline looked like a lion that was lying down. The civil engineers bored through the hill and constructed two tunnels to connect downtown Kowloon with the New Territories. The highway and railway extended through the New Territories to the Chinese border. Hong Kong Island itself was also hilly, the highest point being known as the Peak, an exclusive area with the most expensive properties in the territory. The highest hill though was on Lantau Island at just over 3,000 feet. Lantau Island was located to the west of Hong Kong Island and its northwestern side was selected for the site of the replacement airport for Kai Tak. It was decided that the new airport would be called Chek Lap Kok, and at the time it was the world's largest engineering project as it involved not only an enormous international airport on reclaimed land with two well-separated runways, but also highway and railway links and associated bridges. The whole project was a great success, and it was finished in time for the handover of Hong Kong to the Chinese on 1 July 1997.

The hilly terrain in Hong Kong lent itself to some really good hiking options, and the nature of the territory was such that people needed a complete contrast to the daily living experience of being surrounded by concrete and lots of people. The government wisely decided to reserve certain areas around the territory for recreation and designated them as country parks. Good walks were available, and the parks were described as the lungs of Hong Kong. Litter was unfortunately quite a problem generally, both in the country parks and on the beaches. It was a common sight to see teams of Hakka women, who had come from the neighbouring Guangdong province of southern China, set about collecting and disposing of the weekend's accumulation of rubbish, be it in the country parks or from the beaches.

Hong Kong did boast some quite good beaches, albeit not to compare with the finer beaches of Thailand or Malaysia. The very best beaches could only be reached by boat or a substantial cross country hike and thus their cleanliness and unspoilt beauty could be preserved. As a family we often made that hike to the beaches, Maren and I even camping out under the stars occasionally after the children had left home.

There wasn't a need to learn Cantonese in Hong Kong as it was possible to get by with English, especially downtown. Our local town was called Tai Po, and it had been just a fishing village before being developed. We would go there regularly and Maren would do her vegetable shopping in the local market. It was there that a language barrier could be encountered, so Maren learned the basic numbers and a few words of Cantonese. Markets could generally be split into two categories, those intended for the expatriates and tourists and those intended for the locals. The differences were quite obvious in terms of the products on sale and the state of cleanliness. The markets for the expatriates and tourists were usually stocked with items of clothing and accessories, whereas there was more emphasis on food in the markets for the locals.

The smells in the local markets took a bit of getting used to as great numbers of chickens were compressed into small cages and slaughtered on request. Pork was the other most popular meat, often seen suspended at the side of the road as the taxis went by belching out their trademark black smoke! A special local market attraction in winter was snake soup which was a blend of snake blood and alcohol, guaranteed to keep the cold at bay.

When Maren and I were in Hong Kong, the population was 98 percent Cantonese, the remainder being made up of a wide mix of nationalities. There was a huge disparity between the living conditions of the super rich with their mansions and domestic staff and those who were extremely poor and rooted through the rubbish. Surprisingly there didn't appear to be any jealousy between the two sections of society, the have-nots reckoning that next year would be their lucky year. Having written that, Maren and I saw the emergence of a burgeoning middle class during our years in the territory, well-educated and wanting more than their forefathers had.

The Chinese are extremely superstitious, and there are certain numbers that are lucky and those that can bring bad luck. Two numbers that are considered to be very lucky are 8 and 3, so I guess I did the right thing in the eyes of the Chinese in buying the house as the address was 8, 3rd Street! They are also inveterate gamblers, the clatter of the mah-jong tiles when walking around downtown side streets being almost deafening. Officially the only legal form of gambling was horse racing at the two venues on Hong Kong Island and at Sha Tin in the New Territories. It was said that the total amount of money that was bet on the final race of the Hong Kong season was more than was bet on all the races of the United Kingdom season. For those who wanted some serious gambling a 30 minute jetfoil journey to Macau was the answer with its casinos as well as the attraction of the Portuguese cuisine.

Hong Kong is, of course, famous for its restaurants and everything is available from street side open air eating right through to the top five star experience where you go up in a private lift and your standard of dress is assessed before being taken to your table. There was a well- known building of character in Kowloon called Chung King Mansions which boasted a wide choice of ultra cheap accommodation and eating options in its seventeen stories. The building housed the largest number of guesthouses in Hong Kong with just under 2,000 rooms.

The eating style in the numerous restaurants was mainly curry in the traditional styles of India, Nepal, and Pakistan. The food was generally excellent as long as you didn't pay too much attention to the surrounds enroute to and from your establishment of choice. The same could be said of most of the mid range Chinese and Asian restaurants as the route to and from the toilets invariably went through or near the kitchen and you got an excellent view of the cook stripped to the waist as sweat poured down in the stifling heat and humidity and large flames roared towards the ceiling from around the steaming wok.

Expense apart, Maren and I favoured the character and authentic flavours of the mid range eating options. A particular weakness of the Chinese in Hong Kong was their partiality towards good brandy, or perhaps not so good depending on their position on the social scale. Hong Kong had the highest per capita consumption of brandy in the world, and it was not unusual to see two men enjoying a street side lunch accompanied by brandy by the tumbler. Maren got caught out by this once when she had been invited to attend a Chinese wedding. She was engaged in conversation when she was asked if she would like some wine. She accepted thinking that a glass of wine would be nice with the meal. The served quantity was what one would expect to be given for a glass of wine, but when she took the first sip she got a shock as it was neat brandy!

———◦———

A notorious district of Hong Kong was the Kowloon Walled City which was finally demolished in April 1994. The district had been ruled by triads and organised crime was rampant, the police only entering in large groups. Of course Hong Kong also had its red light district with innumerable bars and night establishments, the infamous Wanchai, but the city was the safest I had ever been to. Expatriates of all ages were generally left alone, even if the Cantonese word for a white person was "Gweilo" which meant "Foreign devil", and we felt that we never had to be concerned about the children being downtown and having to make their own way home once they got to a certain age. It was said that Hong Kong never slept and, having been scheduled for many simulator slots in the middle of the night, I can verify the truth of that statement.

The Hong Kong government took the approach of minimum interference and let the people get on with what they were most interested in and that was to make as much money as possible. Hong Kong was and still is a major global financial centre underpinned by the British legacy of a sound legal system. During our time in Hong Kong there was a flat rate of income tax of 15 percent regardless of income. There were many extremely rich Chinese people in Hong Kong being chauffeured around in high-end Mercedes, but to invest in the property or stock markets required nerves of steel at times! A pronounced property bubble developed while we were there, to the extent that a small car parking space fetched as much as a small apartment in one of the major western cities; later on there was a correction in the order of 60 percent.

One of our neighbours where we lived was obviously extremely wealthy and we heard afterwards that he had been keeping a large amount of physical gold in his house. He had gone to the trouble and expense of getting a sophisticated alarm system installed in the house, the only problem being that it was too sophisticated for his maid from the Philippines. She didn't understand how it all worked, and she decided that she would just leave it switched off! One night the house was burgled, and all the gold was stolen.

Chapter 10

WORLDS OF WELCOME

The world is a book, and those who
do not travel read only a page.
—Saint Augustine

———◦———

We had decided that we would not have a "live in" amah (domestic helper) primarily because of the effect that might have on our children, but Maren did engage the services of a Chinese cleaning lady twice a week. Life established itself into a pattern, and the months and years went by quickly. The children were generally happy in Hong Kong and made friends, both at school and on our estate. Maren got involved with a ladies' group as well as doing volunteer work at a Christian home for mentally and physically handicapped children and adults called the "Home of Loving Faithfulness". She also got involved with the cub pack on our estate for a number of years, becoming Akela (Pack Leader) and enjoying the demands of organising and challenging the boys.

I decided to revisit an earlier interest and bought myself a motorbike for getting to and from work. Given the amount of exhaust fumes, especially in the tunnels, it was probably not the healthiest travel option, but the journey time was consistent and I enjoyed riding again. I somehow managed to get through our fifteen years in Hong Kong without a serious accident, which is quite something when considering the volume of traffic and pedestrians downtown.

One aspect of life that we had not anticipated was the matter of snakes. There were snakes in Hong Kong, some being quite poisonous. We lived in the New Territories and we heard about the large pythons that were capable of consuming cattle. The government had wisely put in place an arrangement whereby if anybody saw a snake they could ring a designated number and a Chinese man would come around on his bicycle with a box on the back. He would then don his gloves and proceed to capture the snake, put it into a sack and then into his box. He would then ride off into the country somewhere and release the snake.

Maren got up close and personal with a poisonous snake one day in our back garden. She was hanging out the washing when she was suddenly aware that she was not alone. She glanced down to see a cobra close by in full strike posture. She then proceeded to race indoors at a speed that defied belief and looked through the glass door to observe the cobra slithering down the side of our house. We called the snake man but the cobra was never found; we were just thankful that Maren had escaped unharmed.

Halfway through our time in Hong Kong we decided to sell our home and take some profit on our house as it had increased in value since buying it. It's hardly ever wrong to take profit, but there was some slight soul searching when we watched the prices more than double within eighteen months of selling—that's Hong Kong! We then moved into a smaller house on the same estate for the remainder of our time in Hong Kong which actually suited our needs better, apart from not having a swimming pool.

———◇———

Inevitably, gliding took a major hit during the years in Hong Kong. Everything was wrong for gliding in the territory: the terrain, the weather conditions, and of course the controlled airspace. I somehow managed to keep in touch with gliding during my periods of leave, one in the United Kingdom summer and one in the Australian summer. I had been made a

Life Member of the RAFGSA on my leaving the RAF, and I made a point of visiting the RAFGSA Centre at Bicester during my leave to the UK, retaining contact with the place where my gliding had begun in 1963.

Maren had supported me in my gliding over so many years and she continued to do so as she realised how much it meant to me. Fortunately Cathay gave a generous amount of annual leave, so we managed to enjoy non-gliding holidays as well. I had been given a couple of gliding names in Japan by Gerhard Waibel, and I wasted no time in making contact with Ichiro Sato who worked for the Japanese Sporting Aviation body in Tokyo. One of the 747 freighter patterns gave a couple of free days in Japan, and I used to shower and change having arrived at the hotel after the all night flight from Hong Kong via Taipei. I would then make my way to the local railway station in Narita to board a train into central Tokyo.

Mr Sato would be waiting for me, and he would drive me to the Japanese gliding centre at Sekiyado. Mr Sato's English was limited, but it was a lot better than my Japanese which was non-existent! I have many happy memories of visiting Sekiyado, although in order to legally fly solo I had to go to Haneda, Tokyo's domestic airport, and be given a "special" medical from an aviation doctor—Mr Sato was very apologetic! I never got to fly cross country in Japan as the rice fields were, of course, totally unsuitable for outlanding. There were other restrictions as a flight plan had to be filed with Air Traffic Control for any cross country flight.

I found the Japanese people to be very hospitable and I was given the use of a lovely guest room for my stays at Sekiyado, the only problem being getting used to sleeping on a rock hard pillow! I really enjoyed Japanese cuisine, and there were many good eating establishments in Narita village. On one of my trips to Sekiyado with Mr Sato, he casually mentioned that there would be a "party" at the end of my visit this time. On the way back into Tokyo, we proceeded to the high rise building where Mr Sato worked, parked in the underground car park, and made our way up in a lift. I was now beginning to feel more than a little nervous as I was dressed in normal casual/verging on scruffy gliding gear.

We walked down a corridor, and Mr Sato ushered me into a large room. I just couldn't believe what I saw! The room was close to full with men dressed in lounge (business) suits and in the centre of the room there was a large table well laden with food and drink. To say that I felt embarrassed would be a gross understatement, but once I got over the initial shock and embarrassment and was able to relax at least to some extent, the evening was most enjoyable. Each gliding club seemed to be represented and, one by one, the representative bowed and gave a brief introduction and description of the club he represented. When that was over, Mr Sato indicated that I should make a speech which I did, my words being translated by somebody who had a good grasp of English. On our way to the railway station afterwards, I gently chided Mr Sato and requested that he give me a bit more notice next time!

Another wonderful memory of Japan was when we set off one morning from the hotel in Nagoya on our crew bus for the airport. After a while I noticed that we were not taking the usual route and I queried this with the driver which got me nowhere as he didn't speak English. Some time later the driver pulled over to stop and I then realised what was going on. It was spring in Japan and he just wanted to show us the most wonderful display of cherry blossom before we left.

———◦———

As I would not be able to pursue gliding in Hong Kong, I decided to dust off an earlier interest and started bird watching. I purchased a decent pair of binoculars and a telescope and was a regular visitor to the Mai Po reserves, a wetland area of international significance, being particularly famous for the large number of migrating waders in spring and autumn. A significant number of rare and endangered species were observed at Mai Po on a regular basis and this attracted serious birdwatchers from all around the world, but particularly from the United Kingdom and the United States.

I spent many happy hours at Mai Po, and after a number of years I decided that Maren should come along and see where I had been spending so many of my leisure hours. I arranged a special one day permit at the best time of the year, and I was utterly amazed when we managed to see no less than three Spoon-Billed Sandpipers in the day. It needs to be understood that the Spoon-Billed Sandpiper is a rare bird whose movements are not fully understood but there is sufficient fascination with the species for birdwatchers to travel halfway around the world with the hope of seeing one of these enigmatic little waders.

Often these international birdwatchers would return home disappointed, but on this one spring day, Maren saw no less than three of them! I tried to explain the significance of what had happened, but I was not sure that it had really sunk in. Mai Po reserve is located in the northern part of the New Territories close to the border with mainland China. As I looked across the mudflats at Mai Po, I looked into China itself; many illegal immigrants used to make their way across the same mudflats using the mud equivalent of snowshoes.

———◄◦►———

The year after we arrived in Hong Kong, I received an invitation to attend a very special annual event in the United States. Barron Hilton, president of the Hilton Hotels Corporation, was an aviation enthusiast and had done some gliding. In cooperation with Helmut Reichmann, he set up the Barron Hilton Cup which was an annual competition based on distance flown. The world was divided into regions and the winners from each region and each glider class would be invited to attend Barron's private ranch in northern Nevada, all expenses paid.

World champions were also invited and so Maren and I headed off to Las Vegas for a very special trip. Initially we were accommodated in the Las Vegas Hilton which was an experience in its own right! The first weekend Barron kindly made his yacht available for his gliding guests, and we were made to feel very honoured as we cruised along on Lake Mead. In the evenings we would be collected from the Hilton and transported in a limousine to enjoy the best show in town from the best seats in the house. When it was time to go to Barron's Flying M ranch, the limousine took us to the steps of Barron's aircraft at the local airport and we walked the short distance from the car to the steps via a red carpet.

The whole experience at the ranch was very special and the hospitality was exceptional. Barron had rented a number of high performance gliders and it was up to the guests as to what tasks they wanted to fly. Early in the morning each day Barron made available a number of activities including fishing, flying in a hot air balloon, and flying in a fully aerobatic powered aircraft. As crews prepared the gliders and positioned them onto the runway, pilots and their guests enjoyed a beautiful lunch under the large awning of a huge RV. After the flights, the crews would again take over the gliders and the pilots would shower before enjoying cocktails with the other guests.

On one occasion I landed out at an airport because it was getting late and I didn't have enough altitude to get over the high ground before the Flying M ranch. Having landed, I secured the glider and was picked up by a helicopter that Barron had sent over so that I could be back at the ranch in time for cocktails! I guess every guest had to pinch themselves periodically to confirm that what they were experiencing was real, but it was obvious that Barron really enjoyed hosting top glider pilots who had come from all around the world—and he generously provided an experience that no guest could ever forget.

———◇———

In 1986, I was invited to fly in the Australian Nationals at Gawler to the north of Adelaide and follow up with running a cross country course before heading over to Benalla for the Pre-Worlds competition. On coming to Hong Kong, I had decided that I had finished with my involvement in World Championships, but Tug Willson had other ideas. He knew that the World Championships were going to be held in Australia in 1987 for the first time since they were held at Waikerie to the northeast of Adelaide in 1974, and he was keen that the two of us should represent Hong Kong. I was not at all keen as I was out of the swim of it all but Tug was very persistent, and I finally gave in.

Gerhard Waibel kindly organised a competitive Open Class glider for me, an ASW22BE, which was based in Germany. The owner, Udo Leidinger, was keen to do some flying in Australia, so we arranged that he would do his flying first and then I would take the glider for the big event. The main problem then was getting the glider out to Australia from Germany. I approached senior management in Cathay Pacific and I was given wonderful support from the chairman, Peter Sutch. He authorised the flying out of the glider in one of the cargo 747s to Australia via Hong Kong. He also authorised a return ticket for Albert so I could have my regular crew chief. I organised a second crew person, Peter Heath, in Australia and both his wife and Maren made up our team. The event itself did not go well for me in spite of a couple of daily second placings, and I ended up in ninth position. I had said to Tug in Hong Kong that this would be my last World Championships whether I came first or last and I meant it.

There were two memorable experiences from the time at Benalla. The first one was during the rest day that the organisation called during the Championships. Maren and I took off for the hills having advised my crew that they would not see us until briefing the next morning; if it was to be a true rest day I needed to have a complete contrast! Enroute we dropped into a café for some lunch and ordered our food. As we waited for it to arrive I couldn't help but notice the photographs hanging on the wall. They were of a man holding different species of decent sized fish, and I asked the lady who brought the food about them. She confirmed that the photos were of her husband and she then asked if I was interested in fishing. I said I was and she immediately asked me if I would like to go fishing that afternoon. I said I would and she arranged for her 11-year-old son to arrange fishing tackle and to go with us for the afternoon!

I just couldn't believe what was happening as we were total strangers and she trusted us with her son. We didn't catch any fish, but that was ok as we had a most enjoyable afternoon. On our return to the lady's house we saw that a barbeque was going with a number of people in attendance. She had invited her neighbours around and, of course, we were invited to join them. After a most pleasant evening, we drove back to the airfield at Benalla having had a wonderful taste of what Australian hospitality can mean.

The second good experience from the time at Benalla was when I landed out quite late one day. I landed safely and made contact with the landowner, Keith Christie. He took me to his house, and I was then able to relay my position back to the championships organisation for onward relaying to my crew. Keith's wife, Judy, then proceeded to organise some dinner for me and in due course my crew arrived. By now it was getting quite dark but Keith and other family members organised vehicles and shone their headlights onto the glider as we de-rigged it and got it safely into the trailer.

It was now late but having had some experience of Australian hospitality I had anticipated Judy's question to my crew, "Have you eaten?" They responded that they had not so we all went back to the house and the roast beef came out again. I invited Keith and Judy to come to Benalla and watch the take-offs one day. They accepted the invitation and Maren and I maintained contact with them when we returned to Hong Kong. Some years later they were on their way to Europe for the trip of a lifetime and they routed via Hong Kong. They had planned a spare day in the territory and Maren and I took great pleasure in showing them as much of Hong Kong as we could in one day. The day ended with our taking them to a non-tourist Chinese restaurant for dinner and towards the end of our meal a noisy fight broke out in the corner of the restaurant and we observed that machetes were involved! Trying to appear unperturbed I declared that we were completely safe and that the best course of action for us was to quietly continue enjoying our dinner. As I write in 2012, Maren and I are still in contact with Judy, Keith having passed on.

—◇—

During the time at Benalla, I was invited to participate in an invitational event in the United States later the same year; so three and a half months after the World Championships, I was in Arizona to fly in an event that was sponsored by Hitachi called "The Hitachi Masters". I flew in John Seaborn's Ventus B; the event was special because of the number of top glider pilots present, including Ingo Renner, George Moffat, Dick Johnson, and Klaus Holighaus. One year later I got to do it all over again, this time in Florida, my crew for both events being Trish Durbin.

Flying in my last competition was the end of an era for me. The competition spark had been ignited during my first event in 1970 and flying competitively had given me so many wonderful memories as well as friendships. I loved so many aspects of competition gliding. I loved the comprehensive preparation that was essential for success; preparing the glider and its equipment as well as personal physical preparation—and the all important mental preparation. The top pilots in each class had similar flying abilities but it was often mental toughness and belief in self that made the difference. I was always naturally competitive and hungry for victory, and I tried to pass on that passion for success to my crew so that we were united in wanting to succeed.

I loved getting myself ready for the day ahead, looking closely at the weather information and thinking about tactics for the task such as the timing of my start. I loved strapping myself into the cockpit and experiencing the gentle fluttering of internal butterflies which was so essential for top performance. I loved the adrenaline rush that came with the start and the pacing of my concentration level over many hours on task. I loved the excitement of the final glide, especially if I knew that I had done well! I loved sharing some of my experiences with my crew as they secured the glider for the night.

I have always flown Open Class gliders in World Championships. There is something special for me about flying with long wings. Logically there are many negative aspects with Open Class gliders: they are heavy and demanding to rig, their manoeuvrability in the air is sluggish, and they are expensive to purchase. Nonetheless, there is a certain magic about looking down those long wings and seeing the elegant curve during a positive pull up into strong lift. Flying with big wings also offers an advantage at the end of the day when faced with a long glide out in still air. Bringing the speed back to achieve best glide, that is covering maximum distance for the altitude in hand, is a wonderful experience as the kilometres go by and the instrument that measures altitude slowly unwinds.

My gliding continued as best I could arrange it, mostly in the United Kingdom and in Australia, although I did get two flights with Udo Leidinger in his ASH25E in Germany and a couple of flights from Hope airport in spectacularly beautiful country to the east of Vancouver. One of the people I had come to know in Australia was Ron Sanders, and he kindly let me fly his ASW20 from Waikerie for a week in January 1989. I had never flown a 1,000 kilometre task, the distance being a challenge and a goal for every cross country glider pilot.

—◦—

January is the best month for long distance flights in southern Australia, and the 25th looked as if it could be a good day so Maurie Bradney, the manager of the centre at Waikerie, got the three of us who wanted to have a go at 1,000 kilometre tasks organised early. The gliders were on the runway by 8.30AM, and I was the first to take off when Maurie reckoned that the temperature had risen enough. The tow was silky smooth, and I released overhead and headed straight out on track. The altitude steadily unwound and there was not a hint of any thermal activity. I was now out of gliding range of Waikerie and committed, thinking less than kind thoughts about Maurie's timing!

Finally, with a suitable paddock selected, I felt some activity as I approached 1,000 feet. The activity turned into a solid thermal, and I congratulated Maurie on his superb planning! When I got to the first turnpoint of my big triangle which was a silo at a small village called Beulah, I discovered that there were in fact two silos. I decided that I would take my photograph of the farthest one and started up the second leg. Conditions were generally good although not as good as hoped for as I flew on towards Hay in New South Wales, my second turnpoint.

I then realised that there was one question that I should have asked Maurie before departure. I had no real experience of seriously long distance flying, and I was wondering what my cut off time should be for turning Hay. I finally decided that 5.15PM would be reasonable, and in due course I turned Hay at 5.10PM! I was now faced with a long final leg of some 400 kilometres, but I did have the advantage of a quartering tailwind. The conditions were mostly blue but progress was ok, and eventually I made radio contact with the other two pilots who were attempting 1,000 kilometres.

They were flying a zig zag type task whereas I had wanted to go for the big triangle. They encouraged me and when I advised them of my position they thought that I stood an excellent chance of completing the task.

I finally climbed in my last thermal, taking it higher than was necessary to make sure of making it back. After a safe landing, I was so tired that I could barely get out of the cockpit! Wendy Medlicott, the wife of Harry Medlicott one of the two other pilots still out on task, the other pilot being Mark Laird, came over to meet me and presented me with the best beer that I have ever had. The flight established a British National record, and I was so happy when Maurie confirmed that the photographs and barograph trace were all good. The next ten years saw a continuation of my gliding, mainly in the United Kingdom and in Australia, although I did enjoy ten days flying at Fuentemilanos in central Spain in 1990. I also enjoyed some flying in New Zealand in 1992 courtesy of British glider pilot Justin Wills (son of Philip Wills) and the late top New Zealand competition pilot Ray Lynskey.

Chapter 11

HOLDING FAST

Go confidently in the direction of your dream.
Live the life you have imagined.
—Henry David Thoreau

———◄◦►———

Although I had kept in touch with gliding and remained safe, I had my sights set on retirement plans and doing a lot more gliding. Having spent quite a lot of time in Australia and come to know a number of people, I felt drawn to the country as a retirement destination. There was also no doubt that my blood had been thinned by the years in the heat and the northern European climate did not appeal. Although I was convinced, Maren was not! She prayed about it, asking God to change her heart if He wanted us to be in Australia. God answered her prayers powerfully, and Maren came to a point of being even keener to go to Australia than I was!

Faith had played a major part in Maren's life ever since she came to faith during her teen years. I had always believed, and my family upbringing involved regular church attendance. Although I had experienced moments that had spiritual significance, I had never known a real "wow" moment that would change my life—that was until 9 October 1993 in Hong Kong.

We had been regular in attending church in Hong Kong as a family, and Maren was a member of a mid-week Bible study group; but I wasn't interested, being a church on Sunday man, and that will do me fine, thank you!

During the northern hemisphere summer in 1993, Maren and I had been on a wonderful holiday in Alaska and I had done a lot of fly fishing with a fairly heavy fly rod. This had done my right elbow no good at all, and I ended up with a bad case of tennis elbow. Maren heard about a forthcoming visit by an evangelist from the United Kingdom, Peter Gammons, who had an internationally known healing ministry, and she tried to persuade me to go along to one of the scheduled meetings. I resisted strongly, but she persisted and, with rather bad grace, I agreed to go along.

During the meeting nothing unusual happened but there came a point when Peter asked everybody to sit or kneel and bow their heads in prayer. At that point he gave an altar call which means inviting all who want to give their life to Jesus to put their hand up. I already believed, and I had no intention of responding to the invitation—but at that moment the power of the Holy Spirit came upon me in a way that almost defied description. I was conscious of powerful surges going through my body, the nearest description in natural terms being as if I had put my hands on a live electrical cable, although that doesn't do it justice. I put my hand up, and others came to minister to me and to pray over me.

There was a huge amount of emotion that evening, and the next day at home I wrote out all the sins that God brought to my mind and took the sheet of paper into the back garden to set it alight. I knew that what had happened marked a new beginning in my life, and I wanted to make a public affirmation in some way. The opportunity came some four years later when Maren and I heard that Peter Gammons would be taking a party from the United Kingdom to Israel—we didn't have to discuss it much before we signed up for the trip.

The visit to Israel in 1997 was special for many reasons, not the least being that I was re-baptised in the River Jordan. Man's rules specify that a person should only be baptised once, but, as for many people, I was baptised as an infant and, of course, could remember nothing of the day.

Now I knew where I stood in my faith, and I wanted to be baptised in public as a declaration of my new beginning.

It is no exaggeration to declare that my life has not been the same since that amazing evening in Hong Kong in 1993. I know who I am in God, and I have the rock solid certainty of where I am going after I leave this earth. It is so wonderful to be part of the family of true believers at last. God knows each of us better than we know ourselves, and He knew that I needed a good shot in the arm to really get me going!

As we approached the end of our time in Hong Kong having made the decision to retire to Australia, I had to address the issue of getting a visa. I made my way over to the Australian Consulate in Hong Kong and pored over all the available information regarding the different categories of visa. I knew that there was a retirement category, but the details of it had changed, and I found that approval was given for only four years, and then further approval had to be sought. I surmised that the subsequent approvals would be pretty much a formality as long as we had funds and had not been in jail, but I didn't like the option as a first choice, so I continued looking.

Finally I came across a category which I felt I could build a case for— the "Distinguished Talent" category. I decided to prepare our case myself having taken advice, and so I put together every bit of information that could possibly have been relevant, including letters of reference from senior figures in the gliding movements of both the United Kingdom and Australia. I deposited the pile of documents on the front desk of the Australian Consulate, and I was advised that it would take six months for a final decision.

Having applied for the visa, there was the small matter of where we were going to settle in Australia! Being confident of the visa application succeeding, Maren and I took a fortnight's holiday in late 1994 and we travelled thousands of kilometres looking for a suitable area. As we headed back north through New South Wales, we dropped into a gliding club which had experienced a major fire to see how they were doing. At the end of the visit we were asked where we were going to from there and we told them that we were going to continue heading north looking for a suitable area for our retirement plans before swinging through Toowoomba (a city of approximately 130,000 just over an hour's drive to the west of Brisbane) to inspect some investment property we owned.

It was suggested to us that we should route through Dalby as a commercial gliding setup had recently started operating there. When I was told the names of the three guys who had set it up, I decided that we would definitely route through Dalby as I knew two of them. When we arrived in Dalby, I was given a glider and went flying while Maren nosed around in town. We shared notes that evening and we both felt that Dalby was different from anywhere else we had been to, with a good feel to the place and full of friendly people. We decided that this could be the area and that we needed to come down again to spend two weeks in Dalby to really check it out.

After six months had passed, I was faced with a dilemma. I knew that I was not supposed to initiate contact with the Consulate, indeed such an action could have prejudiced the outcome of the application. Nonetheless, I just couldn't stand it any longer and I picked up the telephone. Fortunately a very friendly and cooperative Australian female officer responded and, when I had outlined the situation, she asked me what category of visa I had applied under. When I told her, she responded that she now understood why I hadn't been advised of the outcome yet, the reason being that only a very small number of applications are approved each year under that category. She then kindly agreed to talk to her boss on my behalf and, to our great delight, she phoned back the next day to confirm that the application had been approved. Maren and I went out to do some serious celebrating that night!

———◦———

I had a dream about what I wanted to do in my retirement, at least initially. Gliding had meant so much to me over so many decades and I wanted to put something back into the future of the sport. Yes I had been an instructor for many years, but I envisaged being a coach for experienced, highly motivated juniors from the United Kingdom and Australia. I planned on running advanced coaching courses that would last for two and a half weeks with two pilots on each course. I had always been somewhat of a purist in my gliding and had never contemplated having a glider with an engine, but I now realised that if I was to enjoy the independence of operating from my own property, there really wasn't another option.

I decided that the Nimbus4DM, a tandem two seater with a wingspan of 26.4 metres, was probably the right glider for me, but I had never flown one so I decided to request a few continuous days off on my work roster and fly over to Germany to do some test flying. Maren wanted to come with me, so the evening before my first day off we went to the airport with our suitcase only to be told that the aircraft was full and that we would not get on! The next evening we went down again and this time we were lucky. The nonstop flight to Frankfurt was the last movement of the evening before the start of the overnight curfew at Kai Tak.

We had no sooner become airborne than I was aware of a noise from one of the engines on the left side and the aircraft yawing (swerving) slightly. I then noticed an orange light reflecting on the front of our window frame. I advised Maren that I believed that we had lost an engine and that there might be a fire going on back there. Apparently there was something like 200 feet of orange flame coming out from the engine, and observers on the ground thought that the aircraft was lost as it entered cloud and the whole cloud lit up.

I knew the Captain, Colin Baldwin, from RAF days and I was quite relaxed about the whole thing, apart from the frustration of losing another day! Colin and his crew did an excellent job, running multiple emergency checklists and even managing to give two immaculate public addresses before the downwind landing which was carried out some 80 tons over normal maximum landing weight, the landing taking place only 11 minutes after the engine failed. Colin sensibly elected to carry out an autoland with maximum autobrake, and we stopped easily before the end of the runway.

The indications on the flight deck were that the fire was still going and Colin had no choice but to order an emergency evacuation. The cabin crew had done all the preparations and we all went down the emergency chutes; to my amazement the evacuation of more than 400 passengers was completed within 90 seconds. As we were required to leave wallets and handbags on board we had no money to get home, but a kind Hong Kong police officer put his hand into his pocket and gave us the money.

At this point Maren put up the white flag and announced that she had had enough but that I still had just enough time to fulfil the mission. I went back down to Kai Tak for the third time to catch the rescheduled flight to Frankfurt, and this time I made it. I rang the factory from Frankfurt airport to receive the glad tidings from Biggo Berger that it was raining in southern Germany! I proceeded down to the factory anyway not wanting to give up hope, and the workers showed me their newspaper which had a photograph of the Cathay aircraft with its slides deployed. At the back end of the afternoon when it was the early hours of the morning in Hong Kong (my body time), it finally stopped raining, and Tilo Holighaus, Klaus' son who was now running the factory, took me up to the airfield to get airborne. It was all a bit of a blur, but I was alert enough to realise that the Nimbus4DM was indeed the right glider for me, and I confirmed the order. Back in Hong Kong I returned to my normal work routine; but in my leisure time, I was planning the structure of the courses that I intended to run.

Maren and I spent the earlier mentioned two weeks holiday in Dalby in late 1995, and our initial feelings were completely reinforced. We now needed to find the right property, and I did some looking around. I liked one property sufficiently to ask my gliding friend Shane McCaffrey to come out the next day and give it the once over for me. When Shane saw the place, he told me to forget it and go back to Hong Kong as it just wasn't suitable. He agreed to keep an ear to the ground, and if he heard about a place that might fit the bill he would go and have a look at it and give us a ring if he definitely thought it was right.

The months went by and nothing was heard from Shane until one day in June 1996 when I returned from Japan and gave Maren a ring as usual. She asked me if I was sitting down as Shane had just rung and he was very enthusiastic about a small farm that was just about to come onto the market. I told Maren that I would not be able to get away from work for some days. I then checked the passenger loading on the flight to Brisbane that night and, having determined that there was an excellent chance of her getting on, I rang Maren back and told her that she would just have to go down that night as I really didn't want to miss this property. I'm sure I heard tears coming down the phone line, but bless her, Maren finally agreed to go. I was fully aware of the extent of the responsibility that she would be carrying, but we made sure that she would be covered in prayer and off she went.

Shane met her off the coach from Brisbane and took her out to the property the next day to meet the owners and the agent who showed her around the place. That morning Maren prayed that God would give her a clear indication if this was the right place for us to settle. She actually laid down a fleece in that she knew about Australian hospitality and that there would be a break in the proceedings for morning tea. If it was indeed the right place for the Lees, she asked for two things to be in place. The first was that when they went in for morning tea there would be a choice of three different things to eat on the table. The second component was that she would know great peace.

God certainly honoured her request as there were three completely different things to eat on the table for morning tea, and when she looked out the kitchen window at the surrounding countryside, she felt complete peace. Naturally we were keeping in touch by phone, and when Maren told me all of this, I asked her to go for it and try to negotiate a few dollars off the price. I also had peace as I knew the approximate location and I knew that Shane was enthusiastic. Shane was a farmer, and he knew and understood the practical aspects of what I wanted to set up.

I finally got to see our farm some nine months after we had bought it—my colleagues thought I was mad! There was then the question of what we were going to call the property. One day inspiration came to me when I was in the shower; that's it, we'll call it "Plain Soaring", the name being a play on the familiar phrase "plain sailing", as well as reflecting its location on the edge of the Darling Downs plain.

We set about engaging the services of a local property agent and leased the farm to a family who wanted to live on the land. When we came down on our next holiday in 1997 and I got to see the place for the first time, we had a lovely surprise when our tenants arranged a barbeque so that we could get to meet the neighbours.

During this leave we set about selecting a builder to build our new house, but instead of talking to the locals, we naively selected a name from the Yellow Pages and had a meeting with the company owner's wife in Toowoomba. Some weeks after our return to Hong Kong we received a letter from the building company advising us that they were no longer building rural properties, but they recommended another builder from a nearby area.

On our next holiday to Dalby in 1998, I went off gliding while Maren had an initial meeting with the new builder. This meeting went very well and Maren felt comfortable and confident with him. It was sometime later that we found out that he had won the Australian Quality Builder of the Year award for a number of consecutive years! Even though we had approached the builder selection process in totally the wrong way, it had ended up much better than we deserved!

During the last couple of years in Hong Kong, Shane acted as my representative and he arranged for the earthmoving works to commence for the construction of my "airfield", two 800 metre long strips in a "T" configuration, each one being four metres wide. Shane had suggested a layout that he thought would work well and the construction work proceeded smoothly. At the same time, we were in regular contact with our builder as we worked towards agreement on the design of our new house. We had no clear idea of what we really wanted, and we had never been involved with the construction of a new house before so we were relying heavily on the ideas of the builder. He sent us a basic design by fax, and Maren and I pored over it prior to sending it back to him in a somewhat modified state. This toing and froing went on for a long time, as reflected in our phone bills, but eventually we reached a point of agreement with the understanding that construction would commence after our arrival in Australia.

—◁◦▷—

Our years in Hong Kong had been special for so many reasons and in particular we were able to enjoy some great holidays. Now I know that holiday stories are boring for those who weren't there, but I would like to share two memorable experiences. The first one occurred during the early years in Hong Kong when we went on an RV holiday in British Columbia. The children were 10 and 13 years of age and they thought it was really cool to drive around in a large RV. My gliding friend, David Baker, and his wife, Mona, had put us up in their home in a suburb of Vancouver before we set off in the RV; and, as he was the president of the local gliding club at the time, he suggested that we spend the first night at Hope airfield, the home of the club. We accepted the invitation, and the next morning we set off in an easterly direction believing that we would sooner or later escape from the cloud and rain.

Enroute we stopped for a break beside a large lake, and I took the opportunity to grab my rod and set off to do some fishing, Maren and the children choosing to remain with the RV. I picked a spot which was quite a distance from the RV and started fishing, being quite successful in catching some fish. After a while I sensed that I was no longer alone and turning my head very slowly to the right I got a substantial fright when I saw a large brown bear shuffling along towards the water's edge. The bear came by alarmingly close to me, and I just froze while my brain was racing as I considered the options. I reasoned that I could jump into the lake and swim away from danger, or I could throw the fish I had caught to the bear as a peace offering. The bear stopped at the water's edge, sniffed the air for a while, and then proceeded to retrace his steps back into the forest. Now any sane person would sigh with relief and proceed rapidly back to the safety of the RV, but, as a true fisherman, I just let the hairs on the back of my neck settle down again and proceeded to carry on fishing until it was time to continue on with our journey!

The second memorable experience was during a wonderful holiday to South Africa. I had booked accommodation in the famous Kruger National Park, and one day we were driving slowly along a stretch of sealed road in the Park in our hire (rental) car. We were discussing our plans for the day, and I noticed that there was dense undergrowth to our immediate left. As we drove along, the undergrowth suddenly exploded with a large herd of wide-eyed antelope who were apparently being chased by one or more predators. The antelope were fleeing for their lives and they were totally unconcerned by the presence of a four-wheeled metallic obstacle in their way. They continued running and ran all over the car, the noise from the hooves as they clattered over the roof and bonnet being deafening. It didn't seem that it would make any difference whether I braked or accelerated! We never did see the predator(s), but it took quite a while for our hearts to settle down again.

The next part of our travel plans was to drive down to Durban through Kwazulu Natal and then catch a flight down south. It was with a sinking heart that I walked towards the car hire company desk at the airport as I wondered what the reaction of the staff would be to my story. I asked the girl on duty at the desk if she would come with me to the car as there was something I needed to show her. As we walked towards the car I told her exactly what had happened and, to my astonishment, she wasn't at all put out. It seemed that my adventure with the antelopes was not the first time such a thing had happened—all part of living in Africa, I guess!

———<o>———

Towards the end of our time in Hong Kong, I mentioned to Maren that I would really like to take a short break in Japan as I had spent so much time there and it was most unlikely that we would visit the country once we had left Hong Kong. She readily agreed, and I made contact with Mr Sato to see if he could assist us in any way. Well, he did more than just give us some advice; he contacted a gliding friend of his who owned a small hotel in the mountains and he took time off work to come with us and look after us! Japan can be a challenging country to visit once you leave the main cities as signs are only in Japanese and it is more difficult to find people who speak English.

Mr Sato drove us out to the hotel and his wife joined us for part of the time although she didn't speak any English. It was just a great time and gave us such wonderful memories of a country that I had come to enjoy so much. Maren and I both love hiking in the mountains; and although he didn't share our interest, Ichiro would drive us out to a good area and we would meet up again at the end of the day. The small hotel was perfect for us and for much of the time we were the only guests. The four of us would be dressed casually for dinner, but the owner and his wife were formally attired being conscious of their role as hosts.

Two major events occurred before Maren and I left Hong Kong. The first event was the handover of Hong Kong to the Chinese on 30 June 1997. Prince Charles represented The Queen at the ceremony which included a large military presence, the only unfortunate aspect being that it poured with rain and the umbrella to shield Prince Charles was not quite large enough. With effect from 1 July 1997, Hong Kong became a Special Administrative Region (SAR) of China, and Tung Chee-hwa took up his position as the first Chief Executive of the region.

A number of changes took place following the handover, such as The Queen's portrait disappearing from public offices and postage stamps, and British red post boxes either taken away or repainted green. Another obvious change was that the flag of the Peoples' Republic of China was flown alongside the flag of the Hong Kong Special Administrative Region.

Three widely held concerns regarding how life would be post handover related to freedom of the press, freedom of religion, and the fate of the Hong Kong dollar. As far as freedom of the press was concerned, I can only write that there was no discernible difference to press content pre and post handover. Regarding the second concern, a number of churches had made contingency plans to go underground if circumstances required it. In fact no such action was required, and there was complete freedom for people to practice their faith.

As for the Hong Kong dollar, the local unit of currency had been pegged to the United States dollar at the rate of 7.8 Hong Kong dollars to 1 US dollar in 1983 when confidence in the territory's future was at an extreme low. The pegging of the unit succeeded in establishing financial stability, but there was concern that there would be a determined attack by currency speculators on the peg after the handover of sovereignty. In fact, an assault on the peg did take place after the handover, and it proved to be the first major test of the new government. Many wondered how Beijing would react, but a statement issued from Beijing powerfully affirmed confidence in the government of Hong Kong and in particular its Financial Secretary. The statement also clearly made the point that Chinese financial resources would be available if required. In fact, the Hong Kong government successfully fought off the attack, and business magnate George Soros retreated with a bloody nose; the peg remained intact and it still is at the time of writing.

Overall, to all intents and purposes, life in Hong Kong continued very much as before the handover. English continued to be taught in schools, traffic continued to drive on the left, British electrical plugs continued to be used, and the border with China continued to be patrolled.

The second event was when Brian did indeed marry Diana as he had assured us he would! It was decided that the wedding would take place in Budapest in August 1998 and family members joined us from Norway and the United Kingdom. Brian and Diana were first legally married in a government office in Budapest with only close family members present. We then went to a church for a lovely ceremony, and finally on to a military facility for a memorable reception and party, the proceedings including traditional Hungarian dancing. Both the church and the reception venue were located in the historic area of Budapest which gave an extra dimension of occasion.

After the wedding Maren, Sonja, and I went to an historic village in the north of Hungary for a short holiday accompanied by my mother, my sister June, and June's husband, George. We had a wonderful time with many memorable experiences, including managing to inadvertently dock on Slovakian land from a river ferry having used a map that didn't show borders. The armed border guard took our passports away and we discussed the situation, quickly realising that we couldn't drive the hire car in Slovakia, so we elected to stay on the ferry for the return journey. The armed guard, who didn't speak English, brought the passports back and we indicated that we would be returning on the ferry. The guard scratched his head and the ferry Captain rolled his eyes; I got the feeling that they had seen it all before!

Sonja decided to remain in Hong Kong after Maren and I left as she had spent most of her life there and had a lot of good friends, as well as being established in teaching English at a Chinese kindergarten.

On 25 January 1999, Maren and I took off to start our new life in Australia having sent off all our belongings in what we thought would be plenty of time for them to arrive at the same time as we arrived.

About to be baptised
in the River Jordan
in Israel.

The Lee family before
Brian and Diana's
wedding reception.

Chapter 12

Plain Soaring

Those who hope in the Lord will renew their strength.
They will soar on wings like eagles,
they will run and not be weary,
they will walk and not be faint.
—Isaiah 40:31, Holy Bible, NIV

On our arrival, we moved into a motel in Dalby as we were without our furniture and belongings, but we quickly realised that we needed to get onto the farm as soon as possible, for financial reasons at least! A colleague in Hong Kong owned a house in Toowoomba and he kindly loaned us his four-wheel drive vehicle so we would not be without transport initially.

Friends from the local Anglican church rallied around, and we moved into the existing house on the farm with the basics. The very next evening the "storm of a generation" hit Plain Soaring. I was aware of some serious atmospheric activity in the direction of Dalby, and I could see that the storm was heading our way. Shortly thereafter it hit with gale force winds and driving rain, to be followed almost immediately by the electrical power failing. As we sat in the kitchen with our torch (flashlight), we wondered what we had come to.

The next morning I looked out the window and couldn't believe my eyes. The surrounding paddocks looked more like inland seas than fields, and I later learned that 10 inches of rain had fallen the previous night. The construction of our new house was due to commence the day after the storm and a truck actually tried to get up our dirt road but had to turn back. I rang the builder and we agreed a postponement of a week to let everything dry out.

The next drama was our belongings didn't arrive as scheduled. There had been a problem on the high seas, and the ship was still in Singapore—great, what next? The belongings finally turned up some five weeks after the planned date!

The construction of our new house proceeded according to plan, and it was fascinating to be on site and watch it slowly take shape. Six months after commencing the project, the house was finished and we were given the keys. Given that we had no previous experience of building a house and that we had wondered what it might actually look like in reality, we were delighted with the end result. We engaged the services of local contractors to put in the driveway and do the extensive landscaping. The previous owner of the farm had a working piggery but that was not going to be part of our plans so I approached the builder to see if I could come to an arrangement with the man who was doing the heavy machinery work to knock down the piggery buildings, the effluent from the lake having been disposed of before our arrival!

There was one exciting moment while the work was being done. I was nearby attending to some minor tasks when I heard the throttle of the heavy machinery being brought back to idle. I looked over and saw the driver standing on the front of the vehicle looking towards an area of long grass so I wandered over to see what was going on. When I got there the driver just pointed towards the long grass and I could see the bottom half of what had been a large brown snake, the machine having cut the reptile in two. I asked where he thought the other half might be and at that moment the grass parted and the top half appeared, rearing up with its jaw wide open in a very threatening pose. The driver wasted no time in beating a hasty retreat back into his cab and I carried out my own speedy withdrawal.

The brown snake is venomous and is known for its aggression; that was the first of many sightings of snakes on the farm. Maren seems to attract snakes. One day she was outside the house cleaning the windows. It was hot and she was wearing thongs (flip flops) when she became aware of some movement in the area of her feet. She glanced down to see a red-bellied black snake moving across both feet. The red-bellied black, although poisonous, is not as dangerous as the brown snake, but Maren really didn't want one for company. She slowly moved and using the outside broom she tried to steer the snake away from the house. Each time she tried the snake decided that he or she quite liked our house and would start to slither back towards it. Snakes are protected, but Maren had just had enough so she raised the broom and dispatched the snake, breaking the broom in the process!

———◦———

Things had not started too well for me as I was ill when we arrived from Hong Kong, and all I could see was problem after problem. After a while I recovered, but there was a lot of pressure associated with everything we were attempting to put in place. I was feeling a bit down about two months after our arrival, and I was sharing my woes with Paul Appleton who had rented the property while we were still in Hong Kong. He put things in perspective for me when he commented that it wasn't every day that someone retired, migrated to another country, built a new house, and built an airfield. I reflected on his words, and I felt much better!

Other major work projects were also in progress during the time of the house construction. A hangar was constructed over a large concrete slab and the bitumen was laid down on the road base foundation for the two strips. Of course there were various dramas as the projects progressed, such as a major flood washing away the grass seed that had been broadcast on either side of the strips and allowing Texas-sized weeds to get established instead. Overall though, it was very satisfying to see it all take shape.

Just after our arrival, Maren and I set about getting our own transport, and we finally decided to get a utility vehicle for the rough tasks and a comfortable sedan for our travels. Before we arrived in Australia, the glider had been transported from Germany and had been received by the factory agent in New South Wales. A few weeks after our arrival, Maren and I set off in our "ute" to make the long journey down to collect the glider. The return journey was uneventful apart from the fact that it poured with rain most of the time.

It was to be months before I finally got airborne from Plain Soaring, but Peter Griffiths, a member of the local gliding club, owned the same type of glider and he kindly offered to get me airborne so I could recall how to fly as well as keep my enthusiasm level up. The first flight from Plain Soaring finally took place on 29 June 1999 with Shane. I was shocked to see how narrow my four metre wide strips looked from the final turn for landing, but I got used to that quickly. It was so good to get airborne in the first glider that I had ever owned from my own property.

⎯⎯◦⎯⎯

Little by little life began to take shape at Plain Soaring as problems were tackled and overcome. It was wonderful how we were accepted into the local community and, after only a short time, it felt as if we had lived here for years. The farm is about a twenty minute drive from Dalby, far enough to enjoy the advantages of living in the country but close enough to pop into town regularly. We have a good local hospital with the added peace of mind of having two top hospitals and specialists in Toowoomba, just under an hour and a half drive away. It is also just under three hours from Brisbane and just over three hours to the coast when we feel that we need a short break by the sea. Finally, it is a one hour drive to the Bunya Mountains, part of the Great Dividing Range, with rain forest and much cooler temperatures, being some 2,000 feet higher in elevation than Plain Soaring.

I felt that we needed to well and truly settle down before the first gliding coaching course; in particular, I needed a full soaring season to familiarise myself with the operating area. Maren and I continued to attend the local Anglican church, and we made a number of friends; given both our country backgrounds, it was good to be part of a rural community.

Towards the end of 1999, I was advised by the factory in Germany that an engine modification needed to be carried out and that a specialist with his assistant would be flying out to Australia to do the work. They would be based at Balaklava in South Australia, and I had to take my glider there. Initially I thought of driving down, but then I realised that the distance was just too great. My gliding friends encouraged me to fly down; so on 8 January 2000, I took off from Plain Soaring to start the long journey, my only company being a large rucksack strapped in the rear cockpit that was full of personal basics plus a limited amount of engine and glider items. It was a strange feeling as I had no support crew for the first time in my gliding career!

Before leaving, I gave Maren a quick check out on the tractor and slasher so that she could get the grass under control to enable me to land safely on my return. The trip had its exciting moments, but eleven days after leaving Plain Soaring, I landed back just twenty minutes before sunset much to the relief of both Maren and myself.

———◄◦►———

The first of many Plain Soaring courses took place in October 2000. My vision had been to give advanced coaching to experienced juniors from the United Kingdom and Australia—and the first course was successful.

I was pleased with the format and made only minor changes to it over the years. The courses were not just about the flying as I had a ground school syllabus to be worked through as well as a large supply of reading that I wanted each student to complete in his or her spare time. Whilst there seemed to be an inexhaustible supply of experienced British juniors, I found that I had run out of suitably experienced Australian junior pilots after two years, so I started to look at overseas countries.

I ended up hosting six American junior pilots plus three from Austria and one from South Africa, as well as continuing with the British juniors. For my reader who may be a glider pilot, the best task statistics during all the course flying was for a 350 kilometre triangle with Garret Willat from the United States who achieved an average speed of 150 kph and an amazing thermalling percentage of 9 percent.

After five years of pretty well full on coaching of juniors, Maren and I decided that we needed to make some changes. We were getting older, but junior pilots by definition remained within the 18 to 25-year-old bracket! I decided to change the age bracket from the junior range to between 25 and 40 and also to have just one pilot per course instead of the previous two. Instead of the two pilots staying in the original house on the farm, the single pilot stayed with us in the main house. The junior courses reflected my original pipedream, but they were pretty demanding and it was time to back off a bit.

———◇———

The final Plain Soaring course finished in October 2011; it was the end of an era for me. My love of gliding was undiminished, and I could now give my own flying greater attention. The courses had been extremely satisfying, and it was rewarding to see pilots improve during their time at Plain Soaring. It was particularly satisfying to see one of the British juniors, Pete Masson, go on to win the World Club Class Championships at Gawler in South Australia in January 2001. The courses were a team effort, and I couldn't have done them without the unstinting support of Maren for which both our guests and I are so thankful.

I have many happy memories of gliding over the area within which we live known as the Darling Downs. It is a rich agricultural area with dark soil of volcanic origin which is not only extremely fertile but also produces wonderful thermals. Some of the most memorable moments have been sharing thermals with the magnificent wedge-tailed eagle, a large raptor with a wingspan in excess of 7 feet. Their soaring performance is superb and they can easily outclimb a glider, but often they choose to stay with the glider, probably out of curiosity. The most magic of these special experiences is when the eagle decides to fly in formation just off the glider's wingtip. Being at a sub-tropical latitude means that southern Queensland doesn't experience the long days of the southern states, so necessary for the really long distance flights, but on the other side of the coin there is much more soaring available here through the whole year.

Over the years I have had intermittent contact with Hans Werner Grosse, the famous world record setting German pilot, and he has invited me to come and visit him on a number of occasions. In 2007, I decided to take him up on his invitation, and during our annual visit to Germany to see Brian and his family, I travelled to Lubeck in northeastern Germany to catch up with Hans Werner and his wife, Karen. Hans Werner had been a member of a small group of experienced glider pilots who decided to engage the services of a number of experts in the fields of aerodynamics and glider construction with a view to manufacturing a small number of Open Class super-ships. Hans Werner received the first example and I had the privilege of enjoying some magnificent flying in the glider which is called the Eta. There is no restriction on the design of Open Class gliders and the Eta has an extraordinary wingspan of just under 31 metres.

––––⋖◦⊱––––

Gliding has meant so much to me over the past forty-nine years. It was my first flying love and it is now my last flying love. I love the beauty of gliding as shown by the ever changing sky and cloudscape. Each cloud tells its own story, from the small, fair-weather puffy cumulus to the large cumulus that can develop into producing a shower or, in extreme cases, can grow into what is known as a cumulo-nimbus cloud and produce a thunderstorm. I love the different appearances of clouds with the varying sun angles. I love to "read" the sky in the same way an angler reads a stretch of river, even if I'm not airborne! I love the first early glide on a large task in smooth air believing that I will contact the first thermals lower down. I love experiencing the surging power of a strong thermal, and knowing a dream run when it's possible to fly for 50 or even 100 kilometres by linking energy sources without having to stop and climb.

At the other end of the day, I love using the wide smooth thermals as they are by then, followed by the long glide home in air that becomes ever smoother as thermal activity ceases with the sun nearing the horizon. Powered flying is largely about flying from point A to point B so there is a certain predictability about it; whereas with gliding, the pilot is constantly being challenged and making decisions, relying on the forces of nature to complete the task. Even when it all goes wrong and the glider pilot is forced to make an outlanding, he or she can get to meet wonderful people even to the point of making friendships.

Over the years at Plain Soaring I have taken up a small number of passengers, people who have never been airborne in a glider but who have expressed strong interest in doing so. The reactions have varied but I do recall taking up a lady from our church who was very keen to experience powerless flight. I got over to the Bunya Mountains and then managed to climb up above the scattered cumulus clouds. The view was spectacular and my passenger commented that she could see what attracted me to the sport!

———◦———

While Sonja had made a number of visits from Hong Kong to see us, Brian and Diana have made just the one so far. They came in February 2001 and their visit was memorable for more than one reason. When Maren and I purchased the farm, we had seen that there was a dam on the property. When we received some good rain which filled the dam, we naively thought that the supply of water would last us for at least a year to keep our plants going. A few weeks later, the dam was empty and we realised that it had not been properly excavated.

We discussed the choice before us and decided to bite the bullet and get the heavy machinery in. The excavation was nearly finished when Brian and Diana arrived and the job was completed during their stay. Friends of ours lived on a nearby farm and they invited the four of us over to see a different farm and to stay for dinner. As we were enjoying the meal and the company, we became aware that it had started raining and that it was getting steadily heavier. We drove home that night through heavy rain and were quite relieved to make it back safely. The next morning I looked out the bedroom window and I couldn't believe my eyes when I saw that the just excavated dam was full to overflowing. The machinery was still parked around the dam—thank You Lord, You are so good!

Just after Brian and Diana left Australia, Maren and I were made Australian citizens at a ceremony in Dalby. Australia is our home now, and we wanted to make a public declaration of that. Just over two years later, my sister June, and her husband George accompanied my mother on a trip from the United Kingdom to visit us. My mother's health was not good, but she was very determined to come and sample our new way of life in Australia. She was well used to long distance flying as she had often flown to Hong Kong to see us.

After their own holiday at the coast, June and George returned to the United Kingdom and mother stayed on with us for a planned couple of months during our winter season. All was going well until one night she had a nightmare and fell out of bed while trying to switch the bedside light on. Her previously poor back was now in a worse condition, and we had to seek medical attention. One of our local doctors gave her magnificent support, but her stay with us ended up being extended by some six weeks. Despite the setback, I know that she didn't regret making the considerable effort to travel to see us and to get a feel for what our life was like.

The next family event of significance happened in 2006 when we became grandparents with the birth of Benjamin when Brian and Diana were in the United Kingdom. Diana's parents had lived in Germany for many years, and after Benjamin's birth Brian and Diana decided to move over to the same German town where Diana's parents and her brother lived. Brian managed to retain a position as financial manager with a large American company, working from home as well as doing a certain amount of travelling.

The next major event caused a bit of a shockwave! I had just landed from a flight in early 2008 and Maren had come to meet me as usual. As I was unwinding from the demands of the flight before getting out of the cockpit, Maren was pacing up and down proclaiming that she was still in shock. I invited her to share the details of the cause of the state of shock, and she then told me that Diana was pregnant again, but that this time with twins! Anna and Dominic duly entered the world later that year and we then had three grandchildren.

Maren and I realised from the beginning that it was likely we would be separated from Brian and his family, but we reasoned that they could just as easily have ended up on the other side of the world if we had returned to the United Kingdom and that we might as well retire to the country where we wanted to live. Brian and Diana are now fully committed to living in Germany, and they have recently purchased and renovated a house there. I have retirement travel benefits with Cathay Pacific and each year Maren and I make the long journey to Germany and also to the United Kingdom to see June and her family. We travel on a standby basis which is not for the faint-hearted, but it has worked out well for us over the years.

—◦—

Early in 2008 Sonja decided that she was ready to leave Hong Kong, and I engaged the services of a local migration agent. She recommended a particular category of visa for the application and we were told that it could take a year to get the result of the application. The application was lodged in June 2008 and some seven to eight months later we were advised that a case worker had been assigned to her application and that she was to get her police and medical checks done. Everything was on track but there was concern on the part of the Australian government as to the extent of the impact of the global financial crisis and suddenly the decision was made to put a number of visa applications on the back burner. At the time of writing in early 2012, there has been no final decision on Sonja's application.

This was very upsetting for Sonja, as well as for Maren and me, and we all felt that something had to be done. We made the decision that Sonja should come to Australia to study drama and art at the University of Southern Queensland in Toowoomba, less than an hour and a half drive from our farm. She had to come and study as an overseas student, but she is now in her final degree year and she will then do a one year diploma course to learn how to be a teacher. We hope that she will either get a positive response to her original visa application or that she will be sponsored into the country by a school.

The year 2009 was sad as my mother passed away. She had known poor health for many years and she was courageous in the way she suffered a lot of pain without complaining. In 2008 things became substantially worse and over a twelve month period, Maren and I travelled to and from the United Kingdom three times. Mother died just before Easter in 2009, and we had a wonderful service of remembrance in the town where we had owned a house since 1978. At her request, she was cremated and her ashes were taken back to Ireland to be put on my father's grave.

Maren and I decided to sell the house after my mother's death to bring about complete closure, especially for June who lived just up the road and who had so many memories associated with my mother living in our house. We were blessed when a cash buyer came along and fell in love with the house, so we managed to sell the house easily in what was a difficult market.

—◇—

The climate has been interesting since we moved to Australia thirteen years ago. Australia has always been a country of extremes, and the first eleven years were basically years of drought and heat, punctuated by some dramatic storms. Things changed in the beginning of 2011when frequent rain events led to record-breaking flooding over much of Queensland. Some of the scenes shown on TV were dramatic in the extreme. An unexpectedly heavy storm hit Toowoomba after there was already a lot of water every-where, and a powerful river flowed down one of the main streets with cars bobbing along; the whole scene seemed to come straight from a movie set.

Things were particularly bad for a small community about a half hour drive to the east of Toowoomba. It was hard to imagine what the families went through as we watched houses floating along with families stranded on the roofs as they waited to be rescued by helicopter. Central Queensland was also badly hit and tragically many lives were lost through the whole event. Dalby was hit five times, two of them being quite serious with a number of homes being inundated, but thankfully no lives were lost.

Maren and I had not considered the possibility of flooding when we purchased the farm, but the reality is that our house is completely safe from flooding as it is situated in an elevated position on a rocky ridge. The original house is elevated on stumps and is also quite safe. The problem we had when the big flood came was getting into and out of Dalby as amazing quantities of water came across the highway and made the journey quite hazardous. On one day we went into Dalby in the ute to do our Meals on Wheels duty and only just got in. We hoped that the water level would go down during the day, but it didn't and the highway ended up being closed. We spent the night with friends from our church, having purchased toiletries and some items of clothing. We finally managed to get home late the next afternoon.

A farmer and his family who were members of our church and who lived some forty minutes drive from Dalby had been inundated by flood water and we organised a small expeditionary force to go down and help them. A total of some twenty plus houses were flooded in Dalby itself, including our pastor's house when she was on holiday in the United States; another team of church members went around to assist in sorting out her house. A lot of people lost all their possessions, and there were ongoing discussions with the insurance companies about what had caused the flood and whether or not they were actually covered. It is impossible to really get a measure of the impact of flood water until you go to a property that has been inundated and your eyes take in the degree of damage that water can do, as well as the pervading smell that brown flood water leaves.

The next development was that a large amount of donated goods started to arrive and some arrangement needed to be put in place for their distribution. The regional council had arranged with a local company for the use of a huge shed that would be used later for the storage of cotton bales. I put my hand up to organise the relief effort and set about putting a roster together to harness the volunteer manpower to oversee the distribution of the clothing, furniture, and white goods (kitchen appliances). I was overwhelmed by the amount of donated goods and clothing; when we had it all sorted and laid out, it covered a large area of the shed floor. People who came looking for assistance were first interviewed and given a sheet of paper which reflected their specific needs. It was heart breaking to hear the stories, but the relief effort went well, and it was good to know that we were able to help at least some of those in need.

The flood of January 2011 was the worst flood in Dalby since 1981 and the summer season had been declared as being a strong La Nina season. As I write it is the summer of 2011-2012, and the forecast has been for a mild La Nina season, with conditions nowhere near as bad as the previous year. In fact it has been raining for quite a while over the western parts of southern Queensland and northern New South Wales with towns again being cut off. For one particular town, it is the fourth time in two years that it has been flooded. It is devastating for people to go through it all again, but there is a strong Aussie spirit that comes to the fore at such times. The fact is that Australia experiences extreme conditions, both dry and wet, and it has been that way since records began. There are, of course, long-term advantages from big wets for graziers and farmers as the water table gets replenished, but there is a lot of pain involved in any extreme season be it wet or dry.

———◦———

Maren and I have lived at Plain Soaring now for just over thirteen years. A lot of water has flown under the bridge since the problems of the early years, but we have never known such a feeling of home and belonging as we have here. We just know that this is where we are meant to be, at least for the time being. We may not have much contact with our neighbours, but we know that they are there and if there is ever a problem we know that we can count on their help, like the time we managed to lock ourselves out of the house and had to call on our nearest neighbour who happens to be a builder so that we could use his long ladder to climb up and get in through the bedroom window.

The latitude here is very close to what we knew in Hong Kong so the times are familiar for daybreak and twilight. Another thing that we really appreciate is the clarity of the night skies, particularly after the pollution of Hong Kong where we had to really concentrate to see the largest of planets. We have enjoyed some stunning night skies as we are far enough away from Dalby not to be influenced by that light. We have also enjoyed observing some magnificent moonrises, the true beauty of which is almost impossible to capture with a camera. We are both used to country living and the fact that we are 4 kilometres from the nearest main road means that we are seldom disturbed by passing traffic! It's not the extreme quiet that we knew on arrival due to the development of activity in two quarries in the wider area, but it is still very quiet—and that suits us just fine.

We had an entertaining experience a couple of years ago when Mr Sato came to visit us with his son. His son only had a week's holiday and he wanted to see as much of Australia as he could. He spoke very little English, so Mr Sato, who had been to Australia a couple of times, agreed to come with him. I had been inviting Mr Sato to visit us for quite some time and he was keen to come and see us on this trip. I advised him that we were off the beaten tourist track, being just over three hours from the coast, but he was insistent. I also had to apologise to him as my glider was not serviceable at the time so we wouldn't be able to enjoy a flight together, but he remained insistent. Mr Sato let me know that he and his son would be coming to our place from the Gold Coast, so I emailed him detailed navigation instructions on how to get to Plain Soaring. They got to Dalby in good time, but then it all went wrong and they ended up getting horribly lost between Dalby and Plain Soaring, a journey that normally takes twenty minutes. A long time after they were supposed to have arrived, there was a knock on the door. Mr Sato shared with us afterwards that after they realised that they were well and truly lost, he decided that he would stand in front of the next oncoming vehicle to stop it and ask the driver if he knew where George Lee lived. So he bravely stood in front of a large oncoming lorry and proceeded to ask the driver if he knew where George Lee lived; to his astonishment, and certainly to mine, the driver did know and proceeded to give him directions!

———◆———

Sometimes we have visitors who are used to city living and usually one of the first comments made is, "It's awfully quiet isn't it?" and we sense that they are relieved to be going back to the way of life they know. We love the quiet and we love the sense of living in nature. We have a number of different creatures for company, such as kangaroo and wallaby families, echidnas (similar to a hedgehog) and hares. During our thirteen years here we have seen a koala bear just three times as they are very fussy in their eating requirements. It has been noticeable that we have more company when we are undergoing a long period of drought and often kangaroos and wallabies will come right up to the birdbath in our garden. It breaks our hearts sometimes as Mum is having a decent drink but little joey is quite unable to reach up high enough to get his.

We had a fascinating experience once when a family of kangaroos arrived in our garden and it quickly became apparent that Mum was not at all well. She came right up close to the house to let us know that she wasn't well while the younger members of the family and Dad hovered in the background, Dad being a seriously large kangaroo. I had a gliding course going at the time and as we congregated around the dinner table that evening our animal guests positioned themselves close by to let us know that Mum was still not well. It was touching at one point to see Dad gently encouraging Mum with his paw but the next morning they were gone. Mum had obviously recovered and it had most likely been a snake bite.

We also have a healthy bird population and the colours of some of the parrots and lorikeets are stunning. We had a particularly memorable experience one evening when we were enjoying our dinner. I glanced over to the sliding glass door, the bottom of which is nearly at ground level, and I was amazed and delighted to see a barn owl standing by the door and looking in at us with its distinctive heart-shaped face. We love to have the different species of birds but the constant squawking of the young ones in spring can grate somewhat after a bit!

I have a deep love of nature. I was born by the sea and my early years were heavily influenced by that, so I love being by the sea, appreciating its ever changing beauty and distinctive smell. Human beings are drawn to water, and I experience a deep peace when I am by the sea or a lake or a river. We all need to get in touch with our inner self, something that has become difficult with the busyness of modern living, although it is a matter of prioritising how time is spent. I also love the stillness of forests and appreciate the beauty of the shafts of sunlight as they penetrate the top cover, as well as the cocktail of scents that God provides for our enjoyment.

Finally, I love mountain hiking, in particular the physical challenge and exercise, but also the sense of achievement and the magnificent views that await me on the summit.

We enjoy four distinct seasons in the year at Plain Soaring, autumn being the most enjoyable as the days are still pleasantly warm but the nights cool down to assist in getting a good night's sleep. The winter days are also pleasantly warm, but we experience regular frosts at night. Spring and summer can be hot, particularly in the El Nino years, but the humidity is usually low which makes the heat more bearable. The colours of the countryside also change with the seasons; in particular it is beautiful to see the changing colours of the crops, wheat or barley in winter and sorghum in summer. The soil in the region is so fertile that it is possible to enjoy two harvests in the year.

During our years at Plain Soaring, Maren and I have served as volunteers with Meals on Wheels. I have also been invited to be the guest speaker for a number of organisations. I was involved with Rotary for three years, and I currently have a Monday to Friday morning slot on the local community radio station representing the church where Maren and I are elders (leaders). Last year I presented a series of Bible readings on the radio, making comments on what I had read. This year I have started a new series reading Christian books on what God is doing today. I have no idea how many listeners I have, but I do it in faith.

I have always believed in God, but only after my experience in Hong Kong in October 1993 did I realise that my faith had been largely based on head knowledge. That evening turned my life upside down, and I have not been the same person since. Having a personal relationship with Jesus Christ and having a heart that brims over with thanks for what He has done for me and for every person who has lived and will live puts a different perspective on life and particularly on the outlook for the future.

The human life is so short, sometimes tragically so, and where we will spend eternity is of the utmost importance, or it should be. Many people go into denial about death and anything to do with the afterlife, but Christians have the absolute certainty as to what will happen to them after they die. Every human being is a spiritual creature and has a spiritual longing even if many choose to suppress it. Many of those who don't suppress it chase after many different religions and belief systems in an attempt to satisfy their spiritual longing. I just wouldn't have the faith to be an atheist as the evidence for God's existence is all around us.

The theory of evolution has so many holes in it that it just doesn't hold water. We only have to look at the complexities of the human brain, human DNA, the perfection of the universe, and the positioning of our earth giving us just the right amount of gravity for our bodies, not to mention such matters as love, conscience and miraculous healings that cannot be explained. Scientists are not able to prove how life started and they continue to come up against a wall.

Many people accept the case for the existence of God, but if they do there are implications. Why did God create humankind? The Bible makes it clear that God wanted intimacy with humanity, but over the thousands of years, humankind did their own thing and many rejected the God who had created them and who still loves them more than can be imagined.

Jesus bridged the gap that came about between God and humanity due to the original sin, but God gave us freewill, and He will not force anybody to come to faith. Somebody else's faith will not do; we each have to come to our own individual decision—and we will be held accountable for that decision. This is as serious as it gets, and I am unable to understand how anybody can dismiss Christianity without at least thoroughly investigating its claims. I do know this; my coming to true faith in 1993 not only changed my everyday life in a radical fashion, it also gave me an unshakeable assurance for what will happen to me after I die.

My prayer for everybody who reads this book is that they will reach out to God, for assuredly if they do, God will connect with them.

I have lived a privileged and blessed life, but I am not slowing down in readiness for the end. Rather I live in excited anticipation as to what God has in store for me in the years ahead. A recent development was Maren and I being invited to be members of the Queensland State Executive for a new political party called the "Rise Up Australia Party". We accepted the invitation as we agree fully with the goals and principles of the party. As in most Western countries there is much that needs to change in Australia, and it is a privilege to be part of that process.

———◦———

God gave me dreams when I was young, in particular stirring up a hunger for flying. He often speaks to us through dreams and gives us passions—don't push them into a corner. You are capable of accomplishing so much more than you think possible. As you meditate on your passions and what you would really love to do in life, they *will* become reality.

Hold fast to your dreams!

Self and
Australian glider
pilot Craig Collings
during the penultimate
Plain Soaring course.

Maren and I at my
niece's wedding party
in the UK, 2008.

ABOUT THE AUTHOR

George Lee lives with his wife, Maren, on a small farm in Queensland, Australia. He previously flew Phantoms in the Royal Air Force and B747s for Cathay Pacific Airways. Gliding has been a major part of his life. In 1981, he became the first person in history to win three consecutive World Gliding Championship titles. George and Maren have two children, Sonja and Brian, and three grandchildren, Benjamin, Anna, and Dominic.

If you would like to contact the author, please write to:
george.maren@bigpond.com
or visit his website:
holdfasttodreams.com

Additional copies of this book and other book
titles from EVANGELISTA MEDIA™
and DESTINY IMAGE™ EUROPE
are available at your local bookstore.

We are adding new titles every month!

To view our complete catalog online, visit us at:
www.evangelistamedia.com

Follow us on Facebook
(facebook.com/EvangelistaMedia)
and Twitter (twitter.com/EM_worldwide)

Send a request for a catalog to:

**Via della Scafa, 29/14
65013 Città Sant'Angelo (Pe), ITALY
Tel. +39 085 4716623 • Fax +39 085 9090113
info@evangelistamedia.com**

"Changing the World, One Book at a Time."

Are you an author?
Do you have a "today" God-given message?

CONTACT US

We will be happy to review your manuscript
for the possibility of publication:

publisher@evangelistamedia.com
http://www.evangelistamedia.com/pages/AuthorsAppForm.htm